Obama's Seven Deadly Sins

I0104382

-- Second Edition --

Will Americans Forgive or Have Some Tea?

The Seven Deadly Sins of the Bible include pride, gluttony, envy, sloth, lust, greed, and anger. If the US were a religious school and we were trying to teach how to be good, these sins would be on the "not do" list. Only Barack Hussein Obama knows whether he is guilty of any of these sins as a normal human being. The answer to that question is not explored as a personal issue in this book.

These seven deadly sins have had an enormous impact on the moral compass of the ancient world into the modern world. There are traces of these sins in the various interpretations of Christianity, Islam and Judaism. When fully explored, some scholars see even greater significance in these sins than the Ten Commandments as guides in life. Our representative democracy is definitely in trouble with BOH in charge because he has sinned against the American people.

This book identifies his serious flaws as sins and attempts to solve them or prescribe a solution to help get us back on track. Enjoy the book. . As you know, sins can originate from either omission or commission and Barack Obama's Seven Deadly Sins, though surely including some elements of the standard heavy seven shown above are a combination of the two. Maybe one day he will get it right. But, then again, maybe he has never really wanted to. The next President will have it easy being better than this one. America has a lot for which to look forward.

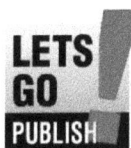

LETS GO PUBLISH!

BRIAN W. KELLY

Published by: ....LETS GO PUBLISH!
Publisher: ....Brian P. Kelly
Editor: ....Melissa L. Sabol
P.O Box 621 Wilkes-Barre, PA
www.letsgopublish.com

Library of Congress Copyright Information Pending
Book Cover Design by Michele Thomas; Editing by Melissa L. Sabol

ISBN Information: The International Standard Book Number (ISBN) is a unique machine-readable identification number, which marks any book unmistakably. The ISBN is the clear standard in the book industry. 159 countries and territories are officially ISBN members. The Official ISBN For this book is on the outside cover:

978-0-9977667-8-3

The price for this work is :   **$10.99 USD**

10	9	8	7	6	5	4	3	2	1

Release Date: January 2010; September 2016

LETS
GO
PUBLISH !

Dedication

I dedicate this book to my big brother, Edward J. Kelly Jr. who was alive and kicking when this book was first printed. Ed is now with the angels. Ed helped me in forming many of the notions brought forth in this book. Ed's research was always right on the mark. While he was doing all that, he was also doing a great Job of being a wonderful big brother.

Thank You Ed!

Acknowledgments

I appreciate all the help that I have received in putting this book together as well as all of my other 65 published books.

My printed acknowledgments had been so large that book readers "complained" about going through too many pages to get to page one of the text.

And, so to permit me more flexibility, I put my acknowledgment list online, and it continues to grow. Believe it or not, it costs about a dollar less to print each book.

Thank you and God bless you all for your help.

Please check out www.letsgopublish.com to read the latest version of my heartfelt acknowledgments updated for this book. Click the bottom of the Main menu!

Thank you all!

Table of Contents

About the Author

Brian W. Kelly retired as an Assistant Professor in the Business Information Technology (BIT) program at Marywood University, where he also served as the IBM i and Midrange Systems Technical Advisor to the IT Faculty. Kelly designed, developed, and taught many college and professional courses. He continues as a contributing technical editor to a number of IT industry magazines, including "The Four Hundred" and "Four Hundred Guru," published by IT Jungle.

Kelly is a former IBM Senior Systems Engineer and IBM Mid Atlantic Area Specialist. His specialty was designing applications for customers as well as implementing advanced IBM operating systems and software facilities on their machines.

He has an active information technology consultancy. He is the author of 74 books and numerous technical articles. Kelly has been a frequent speaker at COMMON, IBM conferences, and other technical conferences.

Brian was a candidate for US Congress from Pennsylvania in 2010

Preface:

This is the second edition of this book

Barack Hussein Obama has committed a lot more than just seven sins against the American people. At least seven of these sins, however are most deadly and one can never know when a huge eighth sin may be delivered by the Sinner in Chief.

In Obama's eight years, Americans have received change, change, and more change. We have received so much change, there seems to no longer be any hope. Even the most change-loving person can only stomach so much change from Washington. It is the attempted change from Democracy to the Obama ideology that has Americans the most concerned.

Thankfully, it will take more than just seven deadly sins to complete a full journey from American Democracy. Yes, seven big sins long ago were put in the Obama ledger but for America to fully disintegrate, many more are still needed. His cohort, Hillary Clinton would be pleased to commit the extra sins needed.

The sins we see all seem to be part of this progressive government with an awful lot of "ism" pie thrown in. The other "isms" are of course socialism, communism, Marxism, Leninism, Fascism and even others. From the President's love affair with the low-ratings media, and the low information voters, it has become a regular happening to see him almost every day taking a bow for something that contributes to our demise. This president loves to campaign, if not for himself, for somebody who he needs to sure up his ratings.

In 2009, for example, President Obama made about five times more campaign appearances than George Bush did in his first year. If the rate of public appearances increased even just a bit more, the country's woes might have solved themselves as Obama would not have any time left to spend in Washington creating harmful regulations. There is a positive side to many negatives.

Why did Brian W. Kelly write this book?

Not too long ago, Brian found himself updating another of his books, Taxation Without Representation, originally penned in 2008 about then current domestic, political, and constitutional issues intertwining the public consciousness. While he was immersed once again in that vortex of all-too-familiar concerns about our government, He felt compelled to add a few paragraphs about the Obama Presidency in light of the transparent failures of the newly coronated Administration.

He wrote at length about many more areas than he expected and before he realized it, the update extended beyond what he would consider a standard update. He knew then that by virtue of its length and current relevance, this work was not a chapter, it actually constituted a new stand-alone book. I am glad that you have elected to join me on this journey. The book of course is "Obama's Seven Deadly Sins."

In the eyes of Americans across the country, from the blue of the mid-Atlantic to the red of the heartland, Barack Obama is failing. Each passing day erodes his declining and oh-so-determinative poll numbers. Said most simply, the man just doesn't get it. He likely never will. Barack Obama does not harbor a thought process anything remotely congruent with the collective consciousness of those he represents, his constituents: US.

Not only has he lost on the domestic front with long discredited socialist policies that would shock Woodrow Wilson, but his domestic failures are not even offset by some countervailing strength in military affairs. National defense under Obama has likewise been weakened. A few more years of Obama's direction, though his heir apparent, Hillary Clinton, fully enabled by a lackluster will doom the country. And I say this… as an optimist

In his eight years as President, he surely has committed more sins than just these seven. But clearly the sins discussed in this book are the seven deadly sins of Obama. And none can be taken lightly.

It takes a lot of sins to make a full "ism." Many know that the Seven Deadly Sins of the Bible included pride, gluttony, envy, covetousness, sloth, lust, greed, and anger. All big sins either are pure versions of one of these seven or are derivatives. If the US were a religious school and we were trying to teach how to be good, these sins would be on the "not do" list.

Only Barack Hussein Obama knows whether he is guilty of any of these sins in their pure version as a normal human being. The answer to that question is not explored in any way as a personal issue in this book. The sins of which we speak are in his running of the United States Government.

The seven biblical deadly sins have had an enormous impact on the moral compass of the ancient world into the modern world. There are traces of these sins in the various interpretations of Christianity, Islam and Judaism. When fully explored, some scholars see even greater significance in these sins than the Ten Commandments as guides in life.

In general, atheists don't use the concept of sin. Since sin in its purest sense is turning your back on God, and atheists do not believe in God, there is no real sin for them. So, something like avoiding the seven deadly sins, with rules about behavior -- stealing, lying, etc. would be something an individual atheist might adopt to help guide their life. From a religious perspective, the seven deadly sins are the worst cases of turning your back on God but they can also be seen as bad acts, even if the act is doing nothing.

So, depending on where President Obama's own moral compass may be set, he might not see the sins noted in this book in a religious context. Sin, according to the thesaurus at Reference.com is many things to many people. None of the things I see in the sin list are good, however. Some of the full and partial synonyms of sin (which include the deadly seven) at this site include the following:

anger	evil	offense	trespass
covetousness	evil-doing	peccability	ungodliness
crime	fault	peccadillo	veniality
damnation	gluttony	peccancy	vice
debt	guilt	pride	violation
deficiency	immorality	shortcoming	wickedness
demerit	imperfection	sinfulness	wrong
disobedience	iniquity	sloth	wrongdoing
envy	lust	tort	wrongness
error	misdeed	transgression	

You can see there is not much wiggle room on SIN when you count the whole list of potential transgressions as shown on the prior page.

As you may know, sins can originate from either omission or commission and Barack Obama's Seven Deadly Sins, while including elements of the standard deadly sins, are a combination of the two. Some sins he commits and others he omits. It is not until you see him act a number of times that you get the sense that in describing what he is going to do, he often omits the part of the story that we might call the plot. Since the plot is the most important part, it has been said that it is far more productive to watch what the President does rather than what he says. There is often a world of difference. Maybe one day he will get it right. But, then again, maybe he does not really want to.

An overriding theme of the Obama presidency that the seven deadly sins seem to reflect is that our representative democracy is definitely in trouble. The President has violated the Constitution in the commission of these deadly sins. In this context, as the lawfully elected executive in the US, he has sinned against the American people.

You may already know that your humble author Brian W. Kelly has written three special books for those who doubt their knowledge of America and the Constitution. They are: *America 4 Dummmies*; *The Constitution 4 Dummmies*; and *The Bill of Rights for Dummmies*. At your first opportunity, please see if you can find a copy of these books, new or used, and read them when you have the time. The books are available at BookHawkers, Amazon, and Kindle.

Beware the lulling idea that your government cannot be overtaken by elected officials, including a strong President and major members of the Congress. Never say "never." Step one is that the word of the people is ignored. What step are we on now? The quickest way to assure that democracy ends and some other form of government emerges is to stop caring and to stop voting and to let those who disrespect our laws have their way.

Brian W. Kelly wrote this book because he cares and I am publishing this book because I care. This book identifies the most notable and serious flaws of the Obama administration to date as characterized by the seven deadly sins. It then attempts to solve them or prescribe a solution to each to help get us back on track.

I hope you enjoy this book and I hope that it inspires you to take the individual action necessary to help the government of the US stand firm against any attacks on democracy from outside or from within this great country.

I wish you the best.

Brian P. Kelly, Publisher
Scranton, Pennsylvania

Chapter 1 What's the Buzz? Tell Me What's Happening!

More Change Than Most Can Stomach

Back in 2009, while, I was updating one of my 75 books, Taxation Without Representation, a book mostly about domestic and constitutional issues, I added a paragraph or two about the Obama Presidency. By then, we were all feeling the effects of this rogue president with a major ideological agenda.

The failures so soon in the Administration were so numerous that I wrote and wrote and wrote. By the time I was finished, I had seven topical areas that I felt were compelling. Before I knew it, my several paragraphs had blossomed into several hundred pages and was too big to be an add-on. The simple addition had become a book by itself. I am glad you have chosen to read it.

President Obama has been failing since early in his first term in the eyes of Americans across the country. His poll numbers began to drop daily and the country was going to hell. He did not get it and now after eight years he still doesn't get it and long after he will never get it – even after he steps down as president. Naming Hillary Clinton as his heir apparent simply proves he does not get it. He doesn't think like us.

Not only has President Obama for eight years been losing on the domestic front big time with socialist policies that would make Woodrow Wilson seem an arch conservative, but he has done one bonehead thing after another that has weakened our national defense. If he were given four more years or if his heir somehow becomes President with a hard left leaning Congress and without changing ways, the country is doomed. And, I am not accustomed to the role of doomsayer.

There may be no "I" in team, but you would swear with the I/Me rhetoric that we have seen domestically and on the international stage, this is a man with the biggest ego in the world and an arrogance matched only by the late Mohammar Quadaffi, Mahmoud Ahmadinejad, and the late Hugo Chavez. You'd swear that it everything for eight years is all about Obama, not the country. That's how he comes across because that's how he goes at it. And, don't think about crossing him.

Unlike President Bush, who while having his own issues, would take the bad pot shots and not raise the rhetoric, I have yet to see anybody from a political pundit, to a news network to a talk show host ever be able to fire a volley at Obama without getting a lightning fast return killer blast. He overwhelmed McCain and Palin after Palin apparently knocked him out at the Republican Convention. He hadn't died nor did he even fall. Whether he is right or wrong, the man does not take no for an answer, and for heaven sake, don't tell him he is wrong. He is a classic caricature of the man who knew it all. He can know no more as he is already filled with all knowledge. His arrogance has no bounds.

I am a Democrat and I did not vote for Barack Hussein Obama because I knew nothing about him. What I knew about John McCain almost made it a draw but I knew McCain would keep us safe and I was and am very worried about having an anachronistic Woodstock cocaine indulging (former) Peacenik running the country. In Obama's own words:

> *"Junkie. Pothead. That's where I'd been headed: the final, fatal role of the young would-be black man. . . . I got high [to] push questions of who I was out of my   mind."*

Obama in the beginning was too young to feel the way he does. But, he does. As noted above, no matter how sound your arguments may be, nobody will change the mind of a man whose intention is to de-nuke the US while, at the same time, permitting Iran to have its way. Don't say that doesn't add up to the man who invented addition.

The first edition of this book came as 2010 was looking us in the face and many of the president's agenda items had passed congress, and that, itself, was scary for me. Now, six years later, as Obama is hoping to pass the baton to Hillary, I am even more scared because Americans know who Hillary is and still many are ready to vote for her. We get the government we deserve.

We Americans are still learning what we have lost with Obama and it may be our entire country. The President accomplished a daunting to-do list in his eight years, and he is hustling to inflict more pain before e is gone. He is clearing Gitmo as we discuss this to keep his last campaign promise, despite those evil guys being happy to kill US all when they are freed.

President Obama spent eight years nudging all US citizens into compliance with his strong will, on the other side of the rope, the high information American People have been pulling like hell, hoping to make up for a double case of severe election mistake.

Obama! Good Man? Good President?

Was this President as nice a man as he originally seemed to be, with many unusually strong and admirable qualities? No sir! He is not cut from the same mold as other respectable Presidents of the United States. There are still about 50% of Americans who disagree with me and they see exactly what I do, and that too has me worried. Their numbers were going down and I thought that was good, Now, they are going up again. What world can those being polled live on?

Again, I must give the President his due credit. He is one of the most tenacious people I have ever observed. He is much more than the spider who kept working to get that first strand across the cave so he could build the web. The spider fell a number of times, brushed himself off, knew he had failed and tried again. Obama never admits failure, never looks beaten, is almost always upbeat, and is always ready for battle. Meanwhile the other side, including me, needs a rest every now and then. He's got a big advantage over most human beings.

Obama Keeps On Going and Going and Going

Like the spider and like King Robert the Bruce, who observed the spider build his web, Obama's motto can be characterized as, "If at first you don't succeed, try, try again." Not a bad motto. However, because he is also the Energizer Bunny, nobody sees him dusting himself off and getting back into the fight. His chutzpah will not permit him to lose or to even show signs of wearing. He can never capitulate. He will not stop until he gets what he wants or he is completely stopped. All of these reasons are included in the many reasons why many admire him.

Because he is such a determined man and he wants so much to achieve goals that I am so much against, he scares me. From my eyes, his agenda must be nipped before the buds turn to flowers and the bad ideas become the strong roots of something that is built to be unmovable. He is not to be taken lightly.

Sarkozy Sees Obama Arrogance

His big weakness is his arrogance and his "me first" attitude. It may be his undoing sometime after his presidency. The foreign affairs honeymoon with the French ended early, for sure, in very late September 2009, at a UN meeting. Obama was well aware that Iran had a second site and had been building nukes for some time there. Nicolas Sarkozy (France) and Gordon Brown (England) knew also and together were ready to dress down Iran's tyrant dictator.

Obama aides cautioned them that this action would look bad because of the President's chairmanship of certain panels and his speech on nuclear disarmament. Brown was more quietly disturbed but Sarkozy was furious. He was somewhat diplomatic, but he called the President "naive and extremely arrogant." He knocked Obama down like he was a little schoolboy. Sarkozy said: "

> *"President Obama dreams of a world without weapons...but right in front of us two countries are doing the exact opposite, Iran since 2005 has flouted five Security Council resolutions, "North Korea has been defying Council resolutions since 1993.*

> *"What good has proposals for dialogue brought the international community?" he asked rhetorically. "More uranium enrichment and declarations by the leaders of Iran to wipe out a UN member state off the map."*

Don't you wish it was our President who was lecturing somebody else about doing the right thing, rather than being lectured about naiveté and arrogance? Don't you wish it was some other country's president who unilaterally canceled defensive missiles in Eastern Europe; did not help the Iranian people on the streets as they were being slaughtered; supported Honduran President Manuel Zelaya against the Supreme Court of Honduras in Zelaya's attempt to be like Chavez and be president for life? Barack Hussein Obama may be tenacious and charming, but he has a few things missing. One of the missing pieces appears to be a deep love of the United States.

Blind Tenacity and Unstoppable Determination

Right from the start, Robert Gibbs, Obama's first press secretary, said that healthcare reform was the Administration's No. 1

priority issue, domestically. We take on the President in this book as this is his seventh and most deadly sin. I was hoping his little vacation in Copenhagen back then would stifle the preoccupation with healthcare, but then I am reminded of his blind tenacity and unstoppable determination.

Since the Obama Administration believes that what it calls healthcare reform, a euphemism for the government takeover of healthcare, requires an Obama hands-on approach, like Arnold, we always know Obama will be back. And, sure enough, there he is on TV the next morning. It was nice even for a day when the salesman in chief on holiday when he snuck off for the weekend to help his buddy Mayor Daly.

He does not hurt us as much when he is away. The question for the times is, "Can Mr. Obama really help the Senate and the House take their five bills and make one out of them?" Like Clinton fatigue in the 1990's, will Obama fatigue be the ultimate killer of this administration as people get sick of hearing the greatest pitch man since Billy Mays RIP.

If anybody can get all five bills together, at least before the fatigue sets in, they are the best salesman in America. Keeping enough votes to get the thing passed may be very difficult if my letters to Congress mean anything. The financier in chief was also scheduled this past fall to be fighting for financial reform legislation on both sides.

Again, Obama is the Energizer Bunny. If he failed on both health care and financial regulation, it would have been an energy miracle for me but a disaster for the hard left. Oh, and by the way, the Senate did not passed cap and trade. But the House, in typical hurry up form, passed it before their summer break way back without taking the time to read it.

2009 Tough Summer for Obama

As difficult it was for those fighting Obama, Reid, and Pelosi on healthcare, it got quiet in the fall 2009, as enemies of the US began to come from nowhere to the UN to be welcomed by our President. In addition to dealing with the prospects of war in Iran, Obama was dealing with winding down the war in Iraq and he was deciding whether the US number one General in Afghanistan was going to get the troops. Of course there was also the little matter of seven prior Attorney Generals of the US at his door and in the media outlets who told him he was screwing up with the CIA inquiries, but on cue, he was not fazed. In fact, he was cheered by kindergarten kids all across the nation on YouTube singing his praises, mmm! mmm! mm! Barack Hussein Obama.

http://www.foxnews.com/politics/2009/09/24/lyrics-songs-president-obama/. Unfortunately, the fine music is not passing the smell test on indoctrination and yet another unneeded battle for the arrogant one is underway.

Oh, and did I mention that he has had second thoughts on Gitmo? I can go on about the foreign policy ills, but this book is about the seven deadly sins of domestic policy. Despite all of the Obama blunders, the corrupt media forgave him in the same fashion as they once punished President Bush. In fact, one of the biggest differences between the Obama presidency so far and the Bush presidency is that George Bush could not make even one little mistake or the corrupt media would nail him as they hung on every single word and twisted it to mean something other than intended.

George W. Bush v. Barack Hussein Obama

Before we close off chapter 1 of this 2-chapter preamble to Obama's Seven Deadly Sins, I want to give some of you a treat. If you still love his arrogance, then you can appreciate how clever the writing is in this email. If you can't quite get your hands on what is wrong compared to the Bush years, in which the low-ratings media told you everything was wrong, this little litany inside this anonymous email that I got in the summer of 2009, with President Obama in office for just seven months ought to help put it all in perspective.

Delivered-To: bkelly(that's me)
Delivered-To: CLUSTERHOST xxxx
X-Spam-Status: No, score=0.0 required=5.0
X-Spam-Level:
From: "Jim Bob" <fallbobr@epix.net>
To: "'Brian W. Kelly'"
Date: Tue, 25 Aug 2009 17:59:26 -0500
X-Mailer: Microsoft Office Outlook 12.0

If George W. Bush had been the first President to need a teleprompter installed to be able to get through a press conference, would you have laughed and said this is more proof of how inept he is on his own and is really controlled by smarter men behind the scenes?

If George W. Bush had spent hundreds of thousands of dollars to take Laura Bush to a play in NYC, would you have approved?

If George W. Bush had reduced your retirement plan's holdings of GM stock by 90% and given the unions a majority stake in GM, would you have approved?

If George W. Bush had made a joke at the expense of the Special Olympics, would you have approved?

If George W. Bush had given Gordon Brown a set of inexpensive and incorrectly formatted DVDs, when Gordon Brown had given him a thoughtful and historically significant gift, would you have approved?

If George W. Bush had given the Queen of England an iPod containing videos of his speeches, would you have thought this embarrassingly narcissistic and tacky?

If George W. Bush had bowed to the King of Saudi Arabia, would you have approved?

If George W. Bush had visited Austria and made reference to the non-existent "Austrian language," would you have brushed it off as a minor slip?

If George W. Bush had filled his cabinet and circle of advisers with people who cannot seem to keep current in their income taxes, would you have approved?

If George W. Bush had been so Spanish illiterate as to refer to "Cinco de Cuatro" in front of the Mexican ambassador when it was the 5th of May (Cinco de Mayo), and continued to flub it when he tried again, would you have winced in embarrassment?

If George W. Bush had misspelled the word "advice" would you have hammered him for it for years like Dan Quayle and potato as proof of what a dunce he is?

If George W. Bush had burned 9,000 gallons of jet fuel to go plant a single tree on Earth Day, would you have concluded he's a hypocrite?

If George W. Bush's administration had okay'd Air Force One flying low over millions of people followed by a jet fighter in downtown Manhattan causing widespread panic, would you have wondered whether they actually get what happened on 9-11?

If George W. Bush had failed to send relief aid to flood victims throughout the Midwest with more people killed or made homeless than in New Orleans , would you want it made into a major ongoing political issue with claims of racism and incompetence?

If George W. Bush had ordered the firing of the CEO of a major corporation, even though he had no constitutional authority to do so, would you have approved?

If George W Bush had proposed to double the national debt, which had taken more than two centuries to accumulate, in one year, would you have approved?

If George W. Bush had then proposed to double the debt again within 10 years, would you have approved?

So, tell me again, what is it about Obama that makes him so brilliant and impressive? Can't think of anything? Don't worry. He's done all this in 7 months -- so you'll have three years and 5 months to come up with an answer.

end of email

Getting those Obama-reminders, one might ask in retrospect, "Was Bush all that bad on foreign policy?" President Bush said repeatedly, back in the spring of 2008, that he would not insert himself into the presidential race. Some still say he lied about that. Others might say that he could not help himself after he took a final trip to Israel.

He was criticized by the left for blasting Iran's President Mahmoud Ahmadinejad as being no better than Osama bin Laden, and they nailed him big time because Bush compared Barack Obama to Nazi appeasers.

May I repeat that? The corrupt media, controlled by the Democratic Party, nailed him big time because Bush compared Barack Obama to Nazi appeasers. Since it was 2008, I must ask, how did Bush even know? It took many of us who gave him a few months to prove himself, every bit of that time to learn that about him. Bush knew because Obama said he would treat Ahmadinejad like any other head of state. Bush knew because he knew Ahmadinejad's secrets.

Bush Took Out the Hammer Early

What a guy. Obama had not even made his whirlwind world apology tour and Bush had him pegged. Coming up is a quite compelling letter that was written during the election time 2008, in the last days of the Bush Administration. Before that, I have a real gem, referenced above, regarding Bush's opinion of Obama that is certainly worth repeating as I introduce and close out the major George Bush part of this book:

> *"Some seem to believe we should negotiate with terrorists and radicals, as if some ingenious argument will persuade them they have been wrong all along, "said Bush, in what White House aides privately acknowledged was a reference to calls by Obama and other Democrats for the U.S. president to sit down for talks with leaders like Iranian President Mahmoud Ahmadinejad.*

> *"We have heard this foolish delusion before," Bush said in remarks to the Israeli Knesset. "As Nazi tanks crossed into Poland in 1939, an American Senator declared: 'Lord, if only I could have talked to Hitler, all of this might have been avoided' We have an obligation to call this what it is -- the false comfort of appeasement, which has been repeatedly discredited by history."*

> *Read more if you choose at:*
> *http://www.huffingtonpost.com/2008/05/15/bush-compares-obama-to-na_n_101859.html*

Before Obama-Times

These are the best of times. These are the worst of times. These are Obama-times.   Some would ask why all this is happening. But perhaps they have not been listening. The sounds are all around us. The following note I received in an email about a letter in the WSJ speaks for many of us trying to ferret out some meaning to all of this in these times:

The below letter was sent to the Wall Street Journal on August 8, 2008 by Alisa Wilson, Ph.D. of Beverly Hills, CA in response to the Wall Street Journal article titled "Where's The Outrage?", that appeared July 31,2008. This is well within the Bush Administration, while the world, at the time, was thinking it might be Hillary or Obama or McCain.

Since Obama had yet to be elected, nobody in America had yet to become outraged by the government's attempt to own this huge industry. The lady who wrote this letter was outraged and was looking for other brave men and women to offer their thoughts. Somebody responded:

Beginning of email

"Really. I can tell you where the outrage is. The outrage is here, in this middle-aged, well-educated, upper-middle class woman. The outrage is here, but I have no representation, no voice. The outrage is here, but no one is listening for who am I?

I am not a billionaire like George Soros that can fund an entire political movement. I am not a celebrity like Barbra Streisand that can garner the attention of the press to promote political candidates. I am not a film maker like Michael Moore or Al Gore that can deliver misleading movies to the public.

The outrage is here, but unlike those with money or power, I don't know how to reach those who feel similarly, in order to effect change. Why am I outraged? I am outraged that my country, the United States of America , is in a state of moral and ethical decline. There is no right or wrong anymore, just what's fair.

Is it fair that millions of Americans who overreached and borrowed more than they could afford are now being bailed out by the government and lending institutions to stave off foreclosure? Why shouldn't these people be made to pay the consequences for their poor judgment?

When my husband and I purchased our home, we were careful to purchase only what we could afford. Believe me, there are much larger, much nicer homes that I would have loved to have purchased. But, taking responsibility for my behavior and my life, I went with the house that we could afford, not the house that we could not afford. The notion of personal responsibility has all but died in our country.

I am outraged, that the country that welcomed my mother as an immigrant from Hitler's Nazi Germany and required that she and her family learn English now allows itself to be overrun with illegal immigrants and worse, caters to those illegal immigrants.

I am outraged that my hard-earned taxes help support those here illegally. That the Los Angeles Public School District is in such disarray that I felt it incumbent to send my child to private school, that every time I go to the ATM, I see "do you want to continue in English or Spanish?", that every time I call the bank, the phone company, or similar business, I hear "press 1 for English or press 2 for Spanish". WHY? This is America , our common language is English and attempts to promote a bi-

or multi-lingual society are sure to fail and to marginalize those who cannot communicate in English.

I am outraged at our country's weakness in the face of new threats on American traditions from Muslims. Just this week, Tyson's Food negotiated with its union to permit Muslims to have Eid-al-Fitr as a holiday instead of Labor Day. What am I missing? Yes, there is a large Somali Muslim population working at the Tyson's plant in Tennessee. Tennessee, last I checked, is still part of the United States . If Muslims want to live and work here they should be required to live and work by our American Laws and not impose their will on our long history.

In the same week, Random House announced that they had indefinitely delayed the publication of The Jewel of Medina, by Sherry Jones, a book about the life of Mohammed's wife, Aisha, due to fear of retribution and violence by Muslims. When did we become a nation ruled by fear of what other immigrant groups want? It makes me so sad to see large corporations cave rather than stand proudly on the principles that built this country.

I am outraged because appeasement has never worked as a political policy, yet appeasing Mahmoud Ahmadinejad is exactly what we are trying to do. An excellent article, also published recently in the Wall Street Journal, went through over 20 years of history and why talking with Iran has been and will continue to be ineffective. Yet talk, with a madman no less, we continue to do. Have we so lost our moral compass and its ability to detect evil that we will not go in and destroy Iran 's nuclear program? Would we rather wait for another Holocaust for the Jews - one which they would be unlikely to survive? When does it end?

As if the battle for good and evil isn't enough, now come the Environmentalists who are so afraid of global warming that they want to put a Bag tax on grocery bags in California; to eliminate Mylar balloons; to establish something as insidious as the recycle police in San Francisco. I do my share for the environment: I recycle, I use water wisely, I installed an energy efficient air conditioning unit. But when and where does the lunacy stop? Ahmadinejad wants to wipe Israel off the map, the California economy is being overrun by illegal immigrants, and the United States of America no longer knows right from wrong, good from evil. So what does California do? Tax grocery bags.

So, America, although I can tell you where the outrage is, this one middle-aged, well-educated, upper middle class woman is powerless to do anything about it. I don't even feel like my vote counts because I am so outnumbered by those who disagree with me.

Alisa Wilson, Ph.D. Beverly Hills, California

There are a lot more out there who think just like Alisa Wilson, the only difference is that she put her thoughts in an email that will reach thousands. Please keep this going and see how big it gets.

GOD BLESS WHAT AMERICA USED TO BE AND COULD BE AGAIN WITH YOUR HELP! SEND THIS ON TO AS MANY AS YOU CAN SEND IT TO AND PRAY THEY WILL SEND IT ON TO ALL THOSE IN THEIR ADDRESS BOOK!!!!!!

-end of email-

I normally understand when I receive one of these heartfelt soliloquies that there is big hurt inside and often I am convinced to feel the same. Most often, I check it out with Snopes (Urban Legends) even though they are a far left leaning source of apparent truth.

Snopes often makes an email author appear to be less than honest and accurate, even if Snopes verifies the speaker who signs the note. In this instance above, Snopes, as liberal and far left as I may have seen them appear in the past, asserted that this note is TRUE. Place a period after this sentence.

Chapter 2   The Government Takeover of the United States

Democracy -- not "Isms"

It takes a tough man to make a tender chicken and it takes a lot of reading to know where I really stand on the big issues. Rod Clark reviewed the first edition of my book, <u>Taxation Without Representation</u> (We are on the Third Edition in 2016) and he had this to say:

> *"Mr. Kelly's political perspective (sometimes progressive, sometimes libertarian) is sometimes difficult to define, and we get a clearer idea of what he is against than what he is for. While Mr. Kelly is more conservative than many Americans (He is among other things an admirer of the "flat tax" and presidential candidate Alan Keyes), he is also an ardent champion of individual rights and the democratic process. He believes that even those dramatically opposed to his ideas should be allowed full and equal access to the democratic process."*

http://www.bookreview.com/$spindb.query.listreview2.booknew.17431

I'd say he's got that right.

Who is President Barack Hussein Obama?

In the two years since the first edition of Taxation Without Representation, a lot has happened in the political / governmental landscape. Barack Hussein Obama, an imminently gifted speaker and champion of change, emerged from virtually no place to take America by storm and with it the presidency.

Most of the first edition of Taxation Without Representation was devoted to Congress and its failure to represent We the People. In the first year of the new President, however, there has been a major power shift to the executive branch, though clearly Congress was complicit in permitting this to happen.

While Nancy Pelosi and Harry Reid march with the gait of hard lefties, President Obama seems to be driving them even further left. In fact, they are so far left and Obama has taken the country so far left that the words Socialism, Communism, National Socialism (NAZISM), Fascism, Marxism, Leninism and even more disturbing "isms" have begun to be associated with this new regime.

Having forty or more Czars (whose counting?), mostly unapproved by Congress, managing or at least directing the spending of literally billions of budget dollars surely does nothing to lessen the impact of all those "nasty" isms. They certainly are not euphemisms or innocuous attempts at humor. Those using these words see a fundamental shift from democracy and it is a bit frightening, to say the least. Most Americans do not believe in that kind of change.

Nobody knew much about Mr. Obama at the outset as his scant service in the US Senate, which was less than a full term. He has no military record. It was difficult to know where he stood on many issues, though his voting record clearly placed him at the very far left. He just did not sound like he belonged way, way on the left.

He sounded like you and I, but he is such a great speaker, he definitely sounded lots better. He is clearly a very convincing man. Coupled with his tenacity and his drive and his high opinion of his own self, he backs down from very little, even when wrong.

After the controversies with his pre-election friends settled down (Reverend Wright et al), he told Americans that they could figure out where he stood on just about all issues by looking at the people with whom he associates. He mentioned Paul Volcker and Warren Buffet as the type of people with whom he associates and by whom he surrounds himself.

The irony is that the idea of judging Obama from his friends and associates was struck down by the candidate himself during the election process, as discussing his pre-election friends was not deemed very productive.

During the campaign, as you may recall, every time then Senator Obama was associated with someone whose views were quite clear, such as Rev. Jeremiah Wright, William Ayers, Tony Rezko, Rev. Michael Pfleger, etc... he was successfully able to disassociate himself from them to the voting public's satisfaction. No, none of these was the kind of person Obama wanted to be known as his friend, or associate, or anything close to him, as he was worried about himself, his reputation, and his personal election opportunities. Yet, that is who he "hung" with. There were not many others who have since emerged as long-time friends.

Get Under the Bus, You're Hurting Me

Some say he threw them all under the bus along with his ailing grandmother, who raised him, for political expediency, and perhaps that describes the best of Obama. Political expediency! In his first year, the new President has convinced the American people that he is just another politician, though perhaps more dangerous.

Besides throwing grandma under the bus in his infamous Rev. Wright speech, don't you wonder why he chose not to visit her? When he finally did visit the woman who "raised him" when his mother could not, just two days before she died, he chose not to bring her grandchildren to see her. Would you do that?

Alone, none of these associations and actions mean anything, but together, perhaps they helped Americans form a much clearer opinion on just where the President stood on a variety of issues, such as friendship and love.

Amidst all the controversy during the campaign, America did not pay attention to the specifics. The low-ratings corrupt media had set the stage that George Bush just was so terrible as president that any Democrat had to be elected or the country would get more of the same. Americans, even long-term Republicans and conservative Democrats wanted change so much that it did not matter.

The Democratic controlled press had poisoned America on anything Bush! Republicans had no chance and any image problems Obama had were masked well by the media. My opinion is that Ripley would have won the election, as long as he was not George Bush -- believe it or not!

Billy Mays Would Be Proud

Moreover, Obama was and continues to be the master salesman. If he did not get elected, he would have been able to step into any of the late, great, Billy Mays exciting TV commercials and outperform the greatest pitch man who ever lived. Can you see President Obama hawking the Awesome Auger or Might Mendit?

Of course that could never be. The country was ready for change so much that a new set of empty clothes would have won the election but no set of clothes could have sold itself as well as president Obama. He is a master. He survived all attacks.

He mounted the most effective campaign that I have ever seen. Though Obama actually ran more against the ghost of George

Bush's past than John McCain, he outclassed and outmaneuvered his real opponent, John McCain, by one lie after another, sworn to by a complicit press. Seniors still have not lose their Social Security but Hillary is now suggesting Trump will be taking it way. It's the same playbook.

McCain Blew It Post Palin

McCain chose to play the gentleman in a fair fight, but Obama had so much pitch-man talent the fight was not fair. McCain showed no fire. Sure, Obama might have had some trouble with that feisty Sarah Palin, however it seemed that John McCain threw her under the bus even before the election for his own reasons, and the corrupt and biased media stomped on her as hard as they could.

It worked well for Obama. McCain really needed everything Palin could bring to the table to beat the political master and grand orator, Barack H. Obama, but Gentleman John did not see it that way. Some postured that McCain did not want to win bad enough. Obama out-Billy Maysed Billy Mays. Obama not only wanted it; he would not take no for an answer.

Disarmament -- The New National Pastime

Thus Mr. Obama became the conquering hero of the American political process. He arose victorious and he became the leader of the most powerful nation in the world. At least, according to most pundits, in 2009, the US was still the most powerful nation on earth. In 2017, when Obama gives up the reins to the next president, the performance in his two terms, especially his very first year may require that US power dominance be fully rechecked. Will we still be # 1?

With disarmament as the new national pastime, will we continue as a superpower? Will the logging and quarrying industries step in to supply the military with enough sticks and stones with which to fight wars? How well we may fare with this President is a big part of the theme of this chapter. Obama found it convenient in his eight years to throw the whole country under the bus and he avoided prosperity like it was a bad thing. After eight years of bad policies, it does not smell very well under the bus.

On September 1, 2009, an opinionated American, whose name is Ken Taylor, commented on the Obama notion of "hope of change," long after the BHO become president. I figured you'd like to hear what Ken, a purported American citizen, felt about the new deal. We don't have a driver's license on file for Ken, so he may very well have been English, or Irish, or Scottish. When you look at Ken's thoughts, please note the rooseveltian reference and the small letters of differentiation.

This is how Ken's post went"

> *"Obama campaigned on the hope of change. After what many saw as a number of "no hope" years, it was an effective message and it was a big reason for the landslide Obama win. Change has come on many fronts and most is not welcomed. "Not that kind of change" is now a rallying cry of many Americans who do not like the push to radical socialism.*

Thank you Ken, for your heartfelt post.

This book. <u>Obama's Seven Deadly Sins, Second Edition</u>. focuses on just a few domestic issues. Somebody else can handle the foreign stuff. Obama's first year gave enough material to write a number of books on what is wrong with our country. Eight years later, in 2016, we would need a multi-volume encyclopedia and then some.

The good ole days I remember now as being just eight years ago, when my biggest complaint was a lack of representation from the "honorables," the Congress of the US. The President then merely got honorable mention. This President, however, has been so radical in his actions (not his words) that he has rallied the bulk of the people in the US, on the right, the center, and even the near left, Democrat and Republican alike, in opposition to the lack of Republic for which he stands.

The Transparency is Opaque

There are a lot of internet search engine hits, that you may enjoy reading, with keywords, "Hope of change" that highlight the lack of representation by the President regarding domestic issues for the last eight years. Don't forget the idea of transparency that was promised by the candidate, but not delivered by President Obama. Watch closely, Transparency means the following according to businessdictionary.com:

> *"Lack of hidden agendas and conditions, accompanied by the availability of full information required for collaboration, cooperation, and collective decision making."*

Is that how you think it has been?

The Road to Surrender

Before I get back on the domestic agenda in the next chapter, I just have to relay to you another piece I found from early September, 2009 when all of us were getting more and more worried about this new President. It is about foreign policy but it also shows something about the leadership of this President and how quickly he would blame George Bush, the blamed one, if he could, or one of his own minions could even if Mr. Bush might be in Crawford TX that particular day barbequing a big moose-sized pig for the neighbors.

This piece is titled aptly, "The Progression of Hope and Change - Obama Attacks CIA, Intelligence Gathering Ends, Terrorists Attack America." Yes, the title could have been abbreviated. Even I, a person who my friends call the "verbose one," could have shortened that title. This is yet another piece from Ken

Taylor's blog at http://www.theminorityreportblog.com.
Nobody knew the early BHO like Ken Taylor. I am now merely
trying to be # 2.

Here are the first two paragraphs:

> *"Raising the white flag of surrender, Barack Obama using
> Attorney General Eric Holder as his surrogate, has begun an
> investigation into CIA interrogation techniques and agents who
> interrogated terrorists. Make no mistake, no matter how many
> times or how many ways that Obama tries to deny his
> involvement or feign opposition to the investigations, the only
> way that Holder has the authority to conduct the investigation is
> with the full knowledge and permission of his boss Barack
> Obama."*

> *"Why does this raise the white flag of surrender? Combined
> with several actions recently taken by the Obama
> administration the clear signal to our enemies is that American
> resolve has weakened and the effort to destroy terrorism is no
> longer a goal or policy of The United States with Obama at the
> helm."*

My son and I had a hearty laugh, just today (2009) as I was
editing this piece, and he tuned into the US that Obama is likely
to leave us when he is gone. I had noted that the loggers and the
quarrymen would create enough sticks and stones to help us arm
the country again, post or concurrent Obama.

We both stopped laughing and started to wonder where we could
find the loggers or the quarrymen. Then we started to muse
about how it would be nice if this is the coming world, that we
knew the two fine folks named Smith and Wesson.
http://www.smith-wesson.com/.

I really am just kidding. But I do thank the Lord that we have the second amendment so that if the government becomes tyrannical, the people have a means of protection.

Moving on from hearty laughs, if you have a particular interest in the foreign affairs of the US, there are a lot of sources on the Internet available by keywords or by large phrases via the many search engines. You can do a lot of your own research to debunk the supposed Obama-truths.

Mr. Obama seems to believe that he can con or perhaps **con**vince the American people into believing anything. Sometimes he does it by pure cunning or in the situation in the quote of Ken Taylor above, he does it by blaming his "George Bush" puppet of the day. "Georgey Bush did it".

This time, on the CIA, of course, George Bush is Eric Holder and Eric got none of the barbeque that day. But, the poor man did get a lot of the heat for trying to bring down a necessary protective agency of our country. Just don't let the CIA, while they are still a US Agency, see Eric Holder enjoying a beer in a local pub.

President's Approval Ratings -- All Time Low!

For a guy who is clearly sharp, the very inexperienced Barack Hussein Obama got into trouble an awful lot as early as his first year as President. I guess we can blame it on OJT (on the job training). Most Americans are very forgiving of the many little faux pas that the President would make because they were not directly affected. To use the words of a good friend, they wanted to "give the guy a chance." The verdict is in and he never should have been given any chances.

When the President began to push hard for action on very important, ground-breaking legislation, so much so that our representatives had no conceivable way of even reading its contents before being rushed to vote, many Americans stopped giving the President the benefit of the doubt. Upwards of 80% of Americans learned that in order for those without healthcare to get healthcare, they first had to (1) give up their own healthcare no matter how good it was, and (2) pay for the healthcare of those previously not covered by increased taxes of unknown but large amounts. After that, they had enough and the benefit of the doubt had worn away. Eight years after the inauguration, Obamacare is still a source of angst and confusion.

In simple terms, only those who were for the President before he made his "CHANGE" and "TRANSPARENCY" arguments are still for his agenda at the close of his second term. Those who were convinced by his campaign rhetoric began quickly to have buyer's remorse. Now that they have observed him governing for eight years, there is no doubt. "What is this guy trying to do?" became the cry of the land.

What was Obama Up To?

Nobody at first seemed to know the Obama secret agenda, but now it is obvious. There was no transparency as promised. What was clear, however is that the visible BHO agenda began to move America so far left that the traditional lefties began to look conservative.

The President has been on his way to complete the molding the US into a nouveau third world non-power wannabee. While he was doing this step by step, or as Cass Sunstein would say, nudge by nudge, people all over America were asking. "Why is he doing this?" Even those who thought he was OK, questioned what their eyes actually saw and their earsactually heard as Obama's nudges continued.

Frustration of Obama

When the American people, not allied to either party, (like me) had really had enough, they wrote their Congressmen / Senators and they waited patiently for the Town Hall meetings promised by Congress in the month of August, during the summer recess. Meetings were held in just about all states of the Union by brave representatives.

It was a tough month for Democrat Representatives who were brave enough to have real Town Hall Meetings. The people, in no uncertain terms, told them they did not want government controlled or government run healthcare. The Democrats felt that they knew better and from the top down, rather than listen to the people, instead, discredited and demeaned them and used the term "angry mob" to describe them.

The Corrupt Media Not Serving the People

There is a lot of American frustration about the fact that there is no free press in America any more. Freedom of the press is gone. Large corporations who benefit from the largesse of government took control of media outlets. Because they are doing so poorly in the ratings wars, and in their financial statements, Dan Rather actually petitioned the US to provide them with bailout funds: Hooey on that!

Only Fox News, ironically owned by an Australian, delivers Americans the news clean and simple, along with conservative opinions, when necessary, to balance the discussion and the churning of the biased media. But Fox is conservative just half of the time.

If it were not for Fox, there would be no honest TV news reaching Americans. We would then have to depend on the corrupt media, once known as the main street media. Their ratings are so poor, that rather than call them the drive-bys as Limbaugh likes to call them or the Fringe Media as Glen Beck has recently labeled them, I like to call it like I see it. They are the low-ratings media for our news and perspectives. Thank God for Fox News.

GE, the largest company in the world, with Jeffrey Immelt in charge of all the toys, owned all the three NBCs -- CNBC, MSNBC, and NBC. How can that be in America?
The NBCs were all big Obama supporters and they have big wallets. They haven't met a piece of propaganda they don't like to spew. See it for what it is. In 2013, however, GE sold out fo $17 Billion to Comcast, who now owns the whole shebang.

Along with the White House and Democratic Leaders in the Congress, all of the NBCs are well in the tank for Barack Hussein Obama, our President, and the rest of his team of CZARS. You get hit with this NBC one-sided stuff in your face when you do not expect it and it sounds real, not like the crap that it is.

On September 8, 2009, I was switching channels and I saw the beginning of the Morning Meeting on MSNBC. There was Dylan Rattigan at the beginning of his morning program putting out a teaser about the town hall meetings, hoping to suck in the channel surfers to stay on and build up the commercial revenue.

"Is this democracy in action or is it just an angry mob!" Rattigan fired that off like it meant nothing to him and it probably does not. He doesn't like the Tea Protestors since the people speak up and his station, MSNBC would rather put them down than give them air time. The good news is that the folks, you and I together, can control the negative voice of Dylan Rattigan. Don't tell him a thing. Don't respond to his on-air dribble. He will get your message by your silence and so will his sponsors.

Look at your family album rather than the illegitimate Morning Meeting. Oh, he'll still be on the air, regardless, but we'll all feel better. He won't be taken off but it will cost GE and Comcast more if they get no people response. He'll still be on the air as propaganda, and the right to control the government's message is very important to GE. I think we can do better than Immelt and Rattigan. Start by changing the channel. Eventually the players change but the din of the liberal progressive beat stays at the core of these network agendas.

The Olympic Blame Game

In October 2009, President Obama, hoping to bring the Olympics back to his "home town" of Chicago, embarked on what some have called the infamous, "Copenhagen Caper." It was such a short trip, the President more than likely had his meals on Air Force One and only his wife Michelle who preceded him on the trip had the opportunity to sample the Danish cuisine.

There was a lot of criticism of this trip. Some blamed Obama for not caring about the US enough. Some saw this as an attempt to bring back a whole ton of political favors to the cronies and the Chicago crowd. Some saw it as a way to heal Chicago more than America as the cost for the Olympics rarely justifies its expense.

I saw it as a nice attempt of the President to bring some prestige to America, whether that was his goal or not. As Mr. Obama in his world confessions tours has diminished the standing of America as a strong and powerful country, and his waffling on foreign issues, and his de-funding of major defense projects, and his tangle with the CIA, has actually weakened America at home and abroad.

I was hoping that we got the Olympics. I had convinced myself that Obama's trip to Copenhagen was a wrap-up on the deal. I would have thought his aides would have prevented a potential embarrassment by knowing ahead of time, whether we were going to get the deal or not. After all, we are America.

There is a lot of humor in this whole story and none better than that captured by John Kass, of the Chicago Tribune, whose tongue in cheek article did not even mention the President. It's hilarious. Here's a quick sample:

> *My loss isn't just financial, it's professional, too. A Chicago 2016 Olympics would have produced seven years of corruption*

stories, seven years of the mayor babbling that he didn't know the guys who got the contracts, even if they're related. So the loss is devastating for columnists and investigative reporters. Why didn't anyone stop me?

Stephanie Avery, writing for the Philadelphia Examiner, noted that George Bush dolls were brought back out of the campaign closets to be picked again for this loss. Poor George, and he thought he was retired:

"Rev. Jesse Jackson blamed it on Bush. This is generally the first sentiment expressed when there is a problem in the world today. Dow Jones is down - Bush's fault; Gas prices are high - Bush's fault; Trillions of dollars in debt - Bush's fault; Hurricanes, crime, divorce, teen pregnancy - Bush Bush Bush. So it is only consistent we blame Bush for the loss of the Olympic bid.

'There must be" resentment against America,' Jackson said. 'The world had a very bad taste in its mouth about us. But there was such a turnaround after last November. The world now feels better about America and about Americans. That's why I thought the president's going was the deal-maker.'

Roland Burris, the Chicago Senator who filled Obama's seat stated that the image of the U. S. is so tarnished even Barack Obama making a personal pitch for the Olympics could not overcome the hatred the world has for us as a result of George Bush.

Maybe Jackson and Burris should be reminded the City of Chicago was announced as a finalist in 2008, while Bush was in office."

Taking a shot at Rush Limbaugh being tickled by Obama's Loss, ABC's Steven Portnoy wrote:

> *"Rush Limbaugh acknowledged his glee in telling his talk radio audience Friday that the International Olympic Committee rejection of Chicago's bid for the 2016 games is a metaphor for President Obama's weakness and an illustration of his 'Mars-sized ego.'*

> *'Who knew the Olympic Committee was a bunch of racists?' Limbaugh joked at the start of his program, saying he was waiting on official confirmation from former president Jimmy Carter, before turning to the gravity of the nation's embarrassment.*

> *'When you stop to think about it, folks, doesn't it make sense?" Limbaugh asked. ' Our president, Barack Hussein Obama, has been running around the world for nine months telling everybody how much our country sucks.... Why would anybody award the Olympics to such a crappy place?'*

> *...'We've got a two-year-old manchild with a Mars-sized ego, which today crashed and burned.'*

> *... The IOC's rejection of Chicago's bid was a 'bitch-slap,' Limbaugh said. 'Upside the head.'*

Despite that we have avoided all the corruption, it does give Americans a good feeling to have the Olympics on our soil. Because it costs so much and so much loot goes in the pockets of ne'er do wells, and because quite frankly, with President Obama at the helm and our record deficits, we can afford no luxuries anymore in America.

So, overall, it is a good thing that the Olympics will not be held in the USA at this time and in Chicago at this time. Now, if we can get on to some serious stuff here (though the blame game does give us pause for some good comic relief).

Yellow Belly Scared Congressional Representatives

There were actually those representatives who were so yellow belly scared to face the people that they used chicanery and subterfuge to pull it off. In Pennsylvania, for example, Rep. Paul Kanjorski, an advocate of government control of healthcare options, could not risk meeting people who opposed his opinion. So, he conducted "Telephone Town Meetings" to avoid the crowd and the voice of the people. He is a clever man. But, representatives of the people should be for the people. What was Mr. Kanjorski for? He never shared it with us other than that he was for whatever Nancy Pelosi said. Thanks Paul. As an aside, I ran against "Kanjo" in 2010 for Congress from Luzerne County in PA.

Sen. Bob [the Weasel], a.k.a. "Acorn Bob " Casey of PA did not begin meeting the people until after he was "refreshed: with a three week family vacation. Bob had no time for the people, but then had second thoughts. Casey decided he should join the party late, and scheduled stealth meetings to minimize the crowd. He could have read right from the bill to the 20 or so fans who came to see him at Lock Haven, PA.

As a PA resident, I did receive Casey meeting notifications via email. He sent emails less than 24 hours before his well-controlled "town hall events." Pennsylvanians knew little about the Casey hidden meetings. Eleanor Rigby was the only one who came. If you had a job, it was pretty tough making arrangements to make it to a Casey meeting with short notice:

Eleanor Rigby (Lennon/McCartney)

Aah, look at all the lonely people
Aah, look at all the lonely people

...

All the lonely people
Where do they all come from?
All the lonely people
Where do they all belong?

Benedict Arlen Specter, RIP, who carried Obama's water through the many Town Hall Meetings he conducted, gained no converts to the government takeover of healthcare. However, he did gain a lot of respect as he took on the tough questions and gave his answers. Unlike Casey and Kanjorski, he stood up like a man and took the bullets and delivered the party line. He made Kanjorski and Casey look like little wimps waiting for Obama droppings to make their day.

Americans came out in droves to the Town Hall Meetings. The TEA Party was at its zenith in 20010. The grassroots American movement was inspirational and unprecedented, but it was not enough to move Nancy Pelosi, Harry Reid, President Obama, Howard Dean and other leaders of the Democratic Party. The party leadership made me ashamed of being a lifelong Democrat.

They said the citizen movement was "Astroturf," a mock on the term "grassroots." They called it a fake gathering of a mob and suggested the Americans who came to the meetings were funded by corporations. They argued that these meetings were not spontaneous reactions of the people to the government trying to force its will on them. They accused their constituents of being liars and malcontents. Yet Pelosi and company did not find it unusual that SEIU and ACORN thugs were bussed in to harass

Americans from exercising their patriotic right to attend these meetings.

As an aside, one of the people identified in November 2009 as having visited the White House the most in these Obama times is Andy Stern, the head of SEIU. Do you think this Union chief and major friend of ACORN has any reason to be looking for favors?

Pelosi, Obama and Reid Insult Ordinary Americans

I keep saying this because it is hard to really believe it happened. Americans protested forced government controlled healthcare and their representatives made a point of belittling ordinary citizens in their ad hoc gatherings because they took the time to tell it like it is. For exercising their rights, they were beaten outside the meetings by thugs. Additionally, these everyday citizens were defamed, insulted, disgraced, and otherwise disparaged by their own elected representatives.

The citizens were rightfully angry to begin with and saw an opportunity to vent their anger by being very animated at the meetings. Once they were put down, citizens became rightfully indignant. The Obama team itself would have none of it. They further encouraged SEIU and Acorn to silence the masses. Since there was no other reason for being there, an honest analysis would show that the busloads of SEIU and ACORN people gave a good demonstration of the meaning of the term, *Astroturfers*.

The Obama and Democratic leadership claims were that these ordinary citizens were all GOP controlled frauds! You and I know that they were people from all parties, like you and I, Independents as well. There were not many from the hard left coming to the meetings to champion their cause and that is why ACORN and SEIU were needed. American citizens who spoke up were independently motivated to do so at these meetings. They did not think in lockstep with the administration and so, in many cases these regular citizens were not welcome at their own congressman's meeting.

That is a pretty tough stance for representatives who long ago stopped representing the people, but who must stand again for reelection in 2016 and 2018. The point is that even if the attendees were organized by the GOP, Republicans and Independents have the right to protest and question their representatives without being called out by their President or Congress. A blog poster named the "Patriarch" added these choice words to describe his frustration:

> *"How dare Obama call them out like this. By calling anyone who is a critic of your plan, an angry mob, or fakes, you are saying that you want no dissent, and that anyone who disagrees with you should not be taken seriously. Pretty soon, the Dems will pass a series of 'Anti-hate Bills' that will limit free speech, and not allow protests of their politicians. Shame on Obama and Dems for what they said about fellow Americans."*

A blog poster named "spinach" offered his or her two cents. Note the tone and you can see the irritation in the masses as reflected by this post:

> *"These liberal nutjobs think that anyone that speaks against them is a criminal. What's funny is these flaming morons are doing more to destroy themselves than the GOP could even remotely attempt to do. These liberal morons are making a whole lot of their OWN VOTERS mad. Kinda poetic, actually."*

The Litany of Obama's Seven Deadly Sins

You may recall the late George Carlin had a fairly graphic shtick about the seven most deadly sins. They were the real bad ones. We won't repeat them here but rest assured they were bad. You don't need to know any more for this chapter than that they were bad. Barack Obama has committed a lot of sins since becoming President. A number of different writers have taken the President to task on things he did on each of his first 100 days calling the acts "Obama's first 100 mistakes," Still others have taken subsets and done some expose's on "Obama's follies." None of these sins are as deadly as Obama's heavy seven!

Though we present this introductory material with a whimsical tone, the fact is that free citizens of the US are coming together to counter what they believe is an attempt to quietly take over the United States Government. That's not funny! The person in charge of this effort is the one-time cheerleader in charge, a man who can rightfully sell ice to the Eskimos, as long as he can get through Sarah Palin up there, of course.

And, on the side, as noted previously, he is revered by those in the business as a better pitch man than the late great Billy Mays. He is undeniably one of the most gifted speakers of all time, especially in government—even better than Bill Clinton. His message is always delivered crisply and saliently. Unfortunately, after he makes the sale, he does not do what he promises. You know what we call people like that but name calling is not important here.

Don't Get Sucked In

What is important is that every American recognize what is happening and tune him out. The man is literally intoxicating, and if you'll pardon my frankness, it is easy to get "sucked back in" once you feel that you have "finally" shed the penchant for Obama. When he is not vacationing, he is on TV every day, sometimes twice or three times for different reasons. When he is vacationing, he is on TV less, but still manages a few cameos. While embroiled in one controversy, he has a knack of getting involved in other controversies, related or unrelated.

Mmm! Mmm! Mm

For example, on September 8, the President planned a little "I love you Mr. President," speech to be given to the Nation's schoolchildren. The children were to be given workbooks so they could list all the ways that they could help President Obama. In Saudi Arabia and in China, when this is done, we call it indoctrination. Before the President got his chance for kindertot full adulation, a bunch of concerned adults shut it down. Angry protests toned down the full propaganda feedback and message, but it took days for the President to release his revised speech.

In the wake of the heavy seven sins, many parents did not want the messenger in chief to spread socialist propaganda to our children. Now that most of his agenda is revealed in the "Heavy Seven," within the first edition of this book, many parents do not want his agenda, period. The last thing a parent needs is to have Little Johnny be lobbying in the kitchen for Barack Hussein Obama while dad is cussing at the TV set.

Obama Fatigue

By the way, don't you think that the more his grace has appeared on National TV, the less believable he became? Even so, there is always the clear and present danger of this great orator gaining control of our minds, even after we may have thought that the spirit had been exorcised. The fact is that more and more citizens distrust his intentions, and more and more are concerned about the power of his band of 40 or more CZARS.

The Pied Piper of Socialism

I was shocked that out of nowhere, or so it seems, in such a short time with him as President, many were getting concerned that Obama's hidden goal was to control every facet of every American's life. Trying this propaganda ploy with our kids strengthens that argument. It did not work fully, but there is always the risk that the youth of America may be attracted to the mesmerizing qualities of this skilled con-artist.

Looking at his record before and after being elected, as scant as the information has been about his "before" activities, Mr. Obama loves the idea of income redistribution -- taking from the rich and giving it to the poor. He is a socialist, of course; but would never dare call himself that because he is a skilled politician. He is against our representative democracy and the Constitution.

His income redistribution schemes and his healthcare redistribution schemes are frightening when seen in this light. These notions are anathema to democracy, and our Republic, but are the friends of all the isms from the totalitarianism of the late Chavez and Castro to Socialism, Communism, Marxism, Nazism Fascism, etc. Nothing in any Obama speech ever indicated any affinity for capitalism and democracy because the top guy does not like the American way. Somebody had to say it. I wonder what his heir apparent, HRC thinks?.

Please Tell Me About the Heavy Seven!

These are not the same seven as George Carlin RIP once promoted in his comedy routines. These are quite serious, and that is the heavy reference. All of the seven issues were from years one and two of the Obama insurgency. OK, I won't make you wait any longer. In simple list form, ladies and gentlemen, these are the heavy seven:

1. The Big Bank Bailouts
2. Indoctrination of US Children
3. The Stimulus, (AKA Porkulus)
4. Economy / Auto Bailout
5. CZARS, Cronies & Snitches
6. Cap and Trade
7. Healthcare

Well, you had to wait quite a while to get at that list. If it looks familiar then, you have been paying attention to the grand excesses of the Obama Administration for almost eight years. They sure do look all too familiar, don't they? As docile as this list appears to be, it was the beginning of many bigger lists that were fashioned to take away more and more freedom from unsuspecting Americans.

To show fairness, Americans were not even offered the choice between one and two-ply toilet paper because only government should make such decision. Cheryl Crow's I sheet per BM trip notion would sure save paper but it might stink up a lot of dining halls.

Can you believe nobody had to wait eight years to find out who Obama was? This stuff was from the very short tenure of Barack Hussein, the 44th President of the United States in his early years. Nobody really knew that damage control would have helped even back then. But, slowing down this tyrant at any stage would have helped and still will. Watch when he is out of office that some Obama time bombs do not go off.

Most of the problem with Obama, as he moves from President to psychological extinction, is that he continued for eight years to think that he was president of the US. He figured as President, he could use his office to create an Obama world. He figured out with a bunch of smart lawyers and law-breakers how to use the rules of a country at random to govern.

It could have been any country but it was our country. The country did not have to be a representative democracy (republic) and it did not have to have a Constitution built into the fabric of the country. Having watched Potter change Bedford Falls into Potterville, through the listed sins and many others, our beloved president tried his darndest for eight full years to change America into Obamaville. Americans simply would not let it happen; but it has gotten much too close for comfort. The Pied Piper has many followers even today!

Figure 2-1 Taxation Without Representation Book Cover

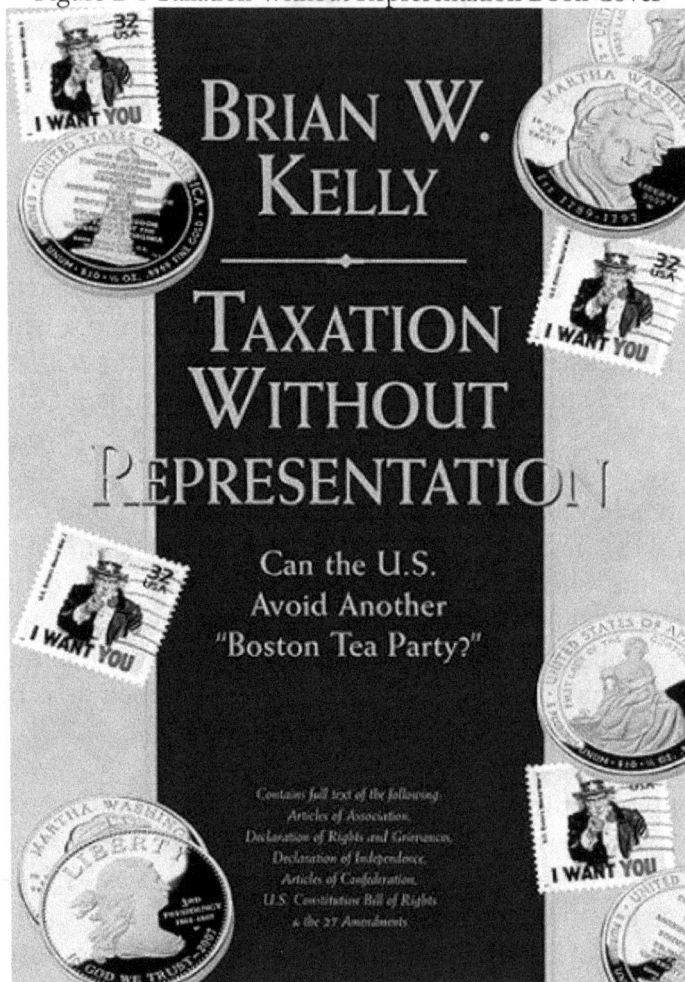

Taxation Without Representation is where Obama has placed us all. He is not representing us in the executive branch and that is why most of us are looking for a real change. The book cover above is the first edition. There was then a 2010/2011 edition, and now there is a Third Edition. The theme is the same but the specifics change. Nobody has ever tried to undermine America as much as Obama has.

Some think that George W. Bush was the worst president ever to befall any democracy—most notably the US. The Iraq war and Bush's pre-disposition to permit big business to gain huge profits off the backs of Illegal Aliens hurt all Americans. Bush continued the Bill Clinton stiffing of the American People by not defending jobs in this country. He made it worse by adopting a policy that the exportation of jobs was somehow good for the American worker. It was all poppycock.

Obama went along like a good soldier. Now, Hillary says she is for Obama policies and offshoring is inevitable. Meanwhile the best businessman in the world, Donald Trump says he will tax their pants off if they manufacture overseas. Yeah Trump!

During Bush's last year I wrote a whole book on the notion of Taxation Without Representation, subtitled, Can the US Avoid Another Boston Tea Party? The cover is shown in Figure 2-1.

Long before the first 2009 "Tea Parties," this book and its concern about the need for true and honest representatives is well documented. It is the story of a corrupt, yet "honorable" Congress and an inept President, whose inability to do the right thing is only trumped by the current President and his administration of despotic CZARS.

Speaking of a lack of performing the people's will, in the rest of this book, we take a hard look at each of Obama's Seven Deadly Sins against the people, one sin at a time, and we acknowledge the complicity of Obama's very well-known predecessor in pulling off the first big sin.

Some sins, such as the idea of a government takeover of healthcare, are so big that we dedicate more words to cover as much of the issue as we can to produce a full picture of the problem while others, though not to be classified as "dinkers" are not laden down with as much detail.

I look forward to exposing the first deadly sin in the next chapter.

The best to you all in fighting this tyranny of Obama, which if Hillary is elected will continue unabated.

Chapter 3 Sin 1 of 7. Bush / Obama Bailouts

The Bailout Season

Looking at Obama sins, we must remember that in 2008, Obama was a newly elected Congressman. Does anybody remember for which platform was he the most excited? What was he against as a Senator and what was he for? Neither can I, and that is why many find him to be very much like the notion of the Manchurian Candidate. What was he against? What was he for?

We all recall that in 2008, during and after the election season, the US began what can be called the US Bailout Season. Between then and now, we spent all the money yet there were no shovel ready projects and the banks are still top of the heap. Hillary Clinton is looking for another $250 Billion were Obama got over $200 Billion. Obama gave the $800 Billion he got to Public Unions and Cronies while Hillary says she will definitely use it for rebuilding bridges. Honestly! She'd swear on a stack of freshly found emails!

Eight years almost from Obama day one and it finally seems like it has ended or will end soon but, this economy has not improved one iota and is nowhere close to stable. In 2008, with the full cooperation of our sitting representatives in both houses, the Congress enacted a series of raids on the people's treasury that was unprecedented in the history of the United States. The country will forever be paying for this poor judgment. It will take so long that it will be our children and children's children who pay the bill, unless China chooses to forgive the bill or maybe just take over the country of which it now seems to own so many pieces. On that very last point, I jest, but it surely is cause for alarm.

Inertia did it!

The laws of inertia document the tendency of a body at rest to stay at rest or a body in motion to stay in motion in a straight line unless disturbed by an external force. That's the physics lesson for today. So, in chronological order, the first deadly sin of Obama was keeping all of the Bush "bipartisan" bailouts in motion. The laws of inertia suggest that if Obama had taken some action to stop the raid, the people's treasury would not have been so pillaged.

Instead he exacerbated the problem by taking even more and turning tons of cash over to cronies. No, it is not all Obama's fault nor George Bush's. Bush is more culpable than one might think as he never stopped the raid on the treasury instituted during the Clinton years.

The big reason for this first set of bailouts was that the government, namely Bill Clinton et al, had demanded that banks be forced to loan mortgage money to anybody regardless of their ability to pay. That's it in a nutshell. In all instances, however, make note that your friendly representatives were complicit. The President can get away with little if Congress is against his or her actions. Republicans and Democrats both let the Clinton banking travesty continue.

Tracing through history we find that Mr. Clinton and many Democrats believed and still believe that everybody is entitled to a home, regardless of whether they ever worked a day in their lives or, if the truth be known, whether they are in the U.S. illegally.

The first home I lived in that was owned by a family member was owned by me. It would have been nice for the government to have given my dad a "don't worry if you can't make the payments loan" so we could have escaped the $25.00 per month rent for our shack on High Street in Wilkes-Barre, PA. Don't think I am kidding. It was only $25.00 per month and worth every penny but not a dime more.

Community Reinvestment Act (CRA)

If you are president, you can make your beliefs happen. So in early 1993, President Clinton ordered new regulations for the Community Reinvestment Act (CRA) of 1977. The effect of the changes increased access to mortgage credit for inner city and distressed rural communities. The new rules went into effect on January 31, 1995. They were great for poor people who had nothing, but because they had yet to have even a little something, like my family, they should have been denied loans and should have lived within their means in $25.00 a month shacks. I lived so why not?

As with many government programs, there was a lot of red tape. For example, banks were required to provide strictly numerical assessments to get a satisfactory CRA rating. Without the proper CRA rating, they were done. Close the bank kinda done!

Though I grew up poor and did not know it, there were no community groups or community organizers like Barack Obama hanging around High Street asking how they could help. The Community Reinvestment Act was first brought forth in 1977, but its provisions became onerous and unfair to the mean old banks in 1993.

Part of the legislation encouraged community groups, such as ACORN, to complain when banks were not loaning enough to a specified neighborhood, an income group, and / or race. This allowed and in fact encouraged community groups to find poor people to take these loans and to extract what I would call a legal extortion "fee" from the banks. Oh, by the way, the Community groups and their organizers were permitted to make a huge profit from the poor in these cases.

Nobody is suggesting that the banks were not the place where there was money. Surely banks had lots of money and a lot of "rich" owners. Before the Clinton work effort of 1993, however, banks were not forced to give up good fiduciary practices and loan to those who, no way, no how, would ever pay the mortgage.

This bubble that burst in 2008, was being inflated first by Clinton, and then Bush who was afraid to stop it. Bush knew that illegal aliens somehow were able to get mortgages for homes they otherwise were not able to afford. Businessman Bush liked the fact that illegal aliens were taken care of in the US so his friends who employed them would be OK. But, he was stiffing the taxpayers and that did not matter to him.

Community Groups Became Important

In the past, banks worried about who you were and whether you could pay back a loan. The Clinton CRA changed that. All of a sudden, banks had to be careful to whom they lent money so their "good citizen" ratings were OK. They had to act according to federal home-loan data broken down by neighborhood, income group, and race.

The data itself was ammunition that encouraged community groups, as noted, such as ACORN, to complain when banks were not loaning enough to a specified neighborhood, income group, and race. ACORN and other in-between groups got extremely powerful and awfully rich.

I need to repeat this in light of the ACORN scandals of 2009. The law actually encouraged community groups like ACORN to market loans to targeted groups and Acorn could make a lot of money by collecting various fees from the banks. Sometimes the fees were, in many ways, bribes for the community group to keep the banks on friendly terms with CRA regulators.

A community group by any other name would be a "business," and some would say a big part of their "business" was extortion, as they more or less preyed on the banks' need for good community relations. What a joke!

My cousin who is a retired executive of a bank, told me first-hand what the new law meant to his bank. Instead of being concerned about the credit worthiness of the borrower, the banks became far more concerned with meeting the CRA guidelines, fearing that the government would basically shut them down if they did not comply.

Noncompliance to these new government "quotas" was not an option. Any bank of any size was either acquiring another bank or being acquired during this period. So, as banks were busy merging, seemingly more often than mice reproduce, they needed to pass the CRA review process in order to be able to continue doing so. If nothing else, this was what banks lived for in the 1990's, and "unbeknownst" to me, groups like ACORN were becoming huge rich entities in the political and financial marketplace, by having a monopoly on extorting banks!

Make Loans to Probable Defaulters Or Else

In essence, the "regulators" imposed an "Affirmative Action" approach to CRA, requiring banks to actively seek out opportunities for CRA loans. In most cases, to book them, bank officers had to relax the credit standards of the bank to get the loan approved. The Feds would include a CRA component in their regular audits, which spooked the banks.

If there were a single complaint about a CRA issue with a bank, the Fed would conduct a separate bank audit just on CRA activity. The threat of a bad CRA audit would not necessarily result in closing the bank, but any mergers, new branches, or branch closings which required Fed approval, would be at risk.

Any bank officer in executive status who was part of doing it cleanly would be out on the street if any of that happened. So, banks were trained to cheat by the federal government. Banks also learned how to minimize their own risk.

None of this could happen with business as usual activities. Banks knowingly had to lower their standards to survive, merge, and to make a profit. Somehow their losses were covered by the taxpayers.

In other words, they substantially increased the number and aggregate amount of credit to low and moderate income borrowers for home loans, many of which were known "risky" mortgages. To be assured of compliance, Banks set up CRA departments. Additionally, this was such a big deal that a CRA consultant industry was created and new financial-services firms helped banks invest in packaged portfolios of CRA loans to ensure compliance.

And, of course in a world in which average Joe's were still not aware of community activism, new community groups began "marketing" such mortgages to the neighborhoods, and taking their cut, modest or not. None of the Community Organizers were without the finest suits and vehicles to assure their acceptance as the "miffintiffs" within the neighborhoods.

In fact, the Senate Banking Committee estimated that as of 2000, as a result of CRA, such groups, which include the infamous ACORN organization, had received $9.5 billion in services and salaries. As of that time, such groups also had received tens of billions of dollars in multi-year commitments from banks for mortgages for their clients.

ACORN was certainly not the only one but they did get their share -- $760 million. There was also the Boston-based Neighborhood Assistance Corporation of America --$3 billion; a New Jersey Citizen Action-led coalition -- $13 billion and the Massachusetts Affordable Housing Alliance -- $220 million and others.

During this period, the number of CRA mortgage loans increased by 39 percent between 1993 and 1998, while other loans increased by only 17 percent. While ACORN et al was hustling the banks, they were also hustling the poor in their communities, as they charged a "nominal" fee in the neighborhood of $100 for their services in getting poor families mortgages, whether the families could afford the $100 or the mortgage, it did not matter. ACORN got paid.

Gramm-Leach-Bliley - Glass Steagall

None of this would have made sense to the Average Joe and so, Joes like yours truly had no idea it was even happening. In addition to Clinton's 1995 actions, there was also some additional help from Congress with a little ditty called the Gramm-Leach-Bliley Financial Services Modernization Act, passed in 1999. This made the problem even worse for banks and strengthened groups like ACORN.

Because the new law offered so many new money-making opportunities for banks, and because President Clinton wanted to assure that the neighborhoods were not forgotten, banks, through our lawmakers, signed up for even more CRA monitoring and more penalties for non-compliance. This law made the CRA ratings assigned by a supervising authority of critical importance to financial institutions.

One of the other "reforms," which contributed to the subprime crisis, under Gramm-Leach-Bliley, was the repeal of the Glass-Steagall Act, a depression era act prohibiting the combination insurance and securities companies.

This was a good act for the people, but the banks never liked it. Under the new law, financial institutions were newly welcome to engage in a financial instrument free-for-all. They could mix and match and combine their businesses in all areas of finance to maximize their returns -- even if it was not good for the stability of their own organizations.

Corporate greed was unleashed big time under Gramm-Leach-Bliley spewing saliva all over one main street bank after another. There was a catch! The banks had to be even nicer than CRA standards to the little guys, the poor, those who had nothing. I don't think my dad would have gone for such crap because he had honor. Besides that, there was no ACORN coming down High Street in Wilkes-Barre, PA ever looking for a nice Irish family like ours to join the fraud party.

Greed hath no bounds. In order to play, banks and other financial institutions acting as banks under the new law had to pay strict attention to the whims of regulators who could withhold authorization for a financial institution to enter into new lines of business, ostensibly based upon its CRA ratings. Surely there were no payoffs for approvals. Banks agreed to get stiffed if the regulators found they were not being nice to the "poor." Eventually, these financial "altruists" cast a scourge on all of us that we are only now beginning to understand.

Whereas it would have been uncomfortable for a bank to move forward with merger plans without taking care of the underprivileged before Gramm-Leach-Bliley, after the passage of this bill, it would be virtually impossible.

Bill Clinton gave away a lot to the big financial firms so as to have none of the neighborhood lending considerations for minorities and the underprivileged scaled away in the bill's passage. Full compliance permitted banks with merger mania to be intimidated since no merger could go ahead without the strict approval of the regulatory bodies responsible for the Community Reinvestment Act (CRA).

Again, groups like ACORN got to be the tattlers, and they would rat on banks that did live up to their promises. They got paid off for their ratting. The greedy banks knew that groups like

ACORN were important long before We the People had any idea that they even existed.

In many ways the original Glass-Steagall Act had kept banks separate from other financial institutions such as insurance companies, brokerage houses, and investment banks. The repealing of this law gave the big financial institutions a free hand in doing anything they wanted to do, without the big hand of government regulation holding them back from huge profits.

Well, not exactly. And to repeat, this was the "rub." To have all the rights afforded by Gramm-Leach-Bliley, a financial institution had to take care of minorities and groups representing minorities in their quest for housing loans, regardless of their ability to pay. Well, not exactly.

Instead of having bank examiners do this work, the government relied on the community organizers, such as ACORN. If ACORN or another "community group" said "no," to a bank, it would cost the bank a ton of opportunity, a ton of profit, and a ton of bottom-line money.

Additionally, for the groups such as ACORN to consider their efforts fully successful, in addition to assuring the CRA requirements, they assured themselves of a nifty stipend to fund ongoing operations. That stipend could have been classified by their accountants as "extortion funds" but, of course, the accountants would be fired.

No bank seemed to consider the amount of that stipend as a deal killer because it was actually the difference between success and failure for the banks. Some may say this helped make ACORN a legitimate shake-down artist? If you would like to shake down the money holders, -- the banks, how convenient it might be to have the federal government as a partner in the crime. Were our representatives sleeping through all of this? Did our representatives get a small finder's fee for being complicit in the defrauding of US Taxpayers?

So, how does anything in this section have to do with Barack Obama? Clearly our representatives gave us up to the big corporations, but did the President have a role? Which President, one or some or all? After all, this stuff all happened under the Clinton Administration and it was fortified under Bush, and then, of course, many of the big bailouts themselves did come from the Bush Administration - even before Obama took office.

So, why is Obama involved. and why is this the background for the "Heavy Seven?" Why is this his first deadly sin? There are two reasons.

The first is that Barack Obama has had an intimate and long-term association with ACORN prior to his major public life. Without a formal card, he is one of them and has admitted as much in speeches. Additionally, ACORN's own Madeleine Talbot knew the promise of Obama and gained his alliance with ACORN.

Under Talbot, and with Obama quietly on the inside, training Talbot's Warriors, ACORN staged "in-your-face" protests in bank lobbies and filed complaints meant to hold up mergers sought by targeted banking firms, unless the banks agreed to ACORN's terms. Eventually, banks no longer even tried to resist. It became a "cost of doing business."

ACORN protests often resulted in their thugs being arrested. Even before Obama, ACORN folks were arrested at banks and other financial institutions making sure they got their due. During the Presidential campaign, Barack Obama kept his distance from ACORN while they took on a role that included bringing in the sheaves, and his team denied as much as they could about his relationship. Yet, when speaking to ACORN in a 2007 speech, as a US Senator, according to Newsmax, the Prez was not shy in asking for help. He had this to say:

"I've been fighting alongside ACORN on issues you care about my entire career. Even before I was an elected official, when I ran Project Vote voter registration drive in Illinois, ACORN was smack dab in the middle of it, and we appreciate your work."

Barack Obama was not just a Chicago Community Organizer, he was a darn good one. OK, he was the best! Nobody asked anybody else to be President. Madeline Talbot, according to the National Review, was so impressed by Obama's organizing skills that she invited him to help train her own staff. Toni Foulkes, who is often documented as a Chicago ACORN leader, admits that Mr. Obama's representation was sought out in a case ACORN filed seeking to force the State of Illinois to comply with motor voter requirements.

Obama Was the Grand Duke of Community Organizing

Obama was active, right after law school organizing "Project VOTE." Foulkes affirms that Obama took this on in direct partnership with ACORN. A few other notable and well known Obama organizing successes were his service on the boards of Woods Fund and the Joyce Foundation. These allowed the young community organizer to help direct tens of millions of dollars in grants to various liberal organizations, which, of course, included the Chicago chapter of ACORN. Incidentally, Obama sought ACORN's support and gained it in his Illinois State Senate race.

So, is Barack Obama responsible for the Bush bailout of 2008, right before the election? Not really! But, his politics are the same politics that use the "Community Reinvestment Act" with input from "Community Organizer Organizations", such as ACORN, to provide positive CRA ratings to cooperative financial institutions. Greed is all powerful, and acknowledging greed is not something unique to Obama. President Bush allowed many of his cronies to suck off the private taps he controlled as well as the public troth. Obama is surely not the first, but he may be the best. The low-ratings media cannot get enough of him.

ACORN's gaining the compliance of banks to issue these "subprime loans" enabled financial institutions to escape the depression era restrictions of Glass-Steagall on "innovation." Please make sure you see the quotes on innovation.

When George Bush and his administration, at the close of his eight years in office, looked at what had been wrought as the price of ACORN et al satisfaction, it was clear that it had big play in the disintegration of the banking industry leading to the federal bailouts of Fannie Mae, Freddie Mac, and others, at the cost of billions of taxpayer dollars.

The CRA and Gramm-Leach-Bliley was the public policy that enabled the market to go corrupt. The banks clearly had survival and profit as their motive. CRA was the driver that pushed them over the edge. Wall Street and investment banks were complicit but not the only ones culpable. All they did was buy up all the risky mortgages that became so prevalent in the market place. Maybe they did not know how bad they were. [I really can't believe that.]

One thing is for sure no matter what happened, no one intended to lose money, and though free capitalism needs to take on part of the blame, the real source of the problem was government in the first place, and then the ugly hand of government willing to pay the cost of greed. Banks should have failed and Congressmen should have been impeached. If you think this was right, then perhaps a bit of remedial fundamental economics is in order.

To understand the magnitude of the financial collapse, let's look at some specifics:

Bear Stearns Early 2008

The first financial institution, of significance, to fail was Bear Stearns. Through the Spring 2008, the end was looming, even after a quick loan from the Fed to keep the company going. Over one weekend, The US Treasury saw that Bear Stearns was going to fail and so Treasury Secretary Henry Paulson and Fed Chairman Ben Bernanke swiftly made a house call on Bear Stearns' CEO Alan Schwartz. They let him know in no uncertain terms that time was up. Schwartz had to sell the company before the end of the weekend with some help from the Fed. Sounds like Obama, but it was Bush.

On the other side of the disaster was JP Morgan Chase and the federal government. Together, using taxpayer money, they bailed out Bear Stearns to avoid the financial giant's collapse. JP Morgan originally purchased Bear Stearns for $236 million (about $2.00 per share) and the Fed gave a $30 billion credit line (our taxpayer money) to ensure the sale could move forward.

Later, after a shareholder revolt and lawsuit on May 29, 2008, Bear Stearns shareholders approved the sale to JPMorgan Chase at a $10-per-share price (about $1.2 Billion). If the name Bear Stearns were Goldman Sachs, where at least seven of the US Treasury Secretaries have hailed, would the company have dissipated? The answer to that questions demonstrates the filth on the hands of the government in these bailouts. Goldman Sachs clearly was immune by its government connections.

Housing & Economic Recovery Act of 2008

In the area of mortgage reform, think of the Housing and Economic Recovery Act of 2008 -- passed July 30, 2008, right before the break, HR 3221. Among some other things, the purpose of this bill was to increase finance industry regulation and help some homeowners at risk of foreclosure. Among its key provisions was to make sure that the government-sponsored home loan agencies (Freddie and Fannie) would never run out of money. In essence this placed the U.S. Treasury (and its ability to print money) in the service of Freddie Mac and Fannie Mae -- the two home loan banks that either owned or insured at least half the loans made to U.S. homebuyers.

In other words, the act assured prospective investors and homebuyers that the U.S. home loan industry's doors would be open for business even if the rest of the economy shut down. It is a taxpayer bailout involving many billions of dollars if the entities fail. Those lousy loans the banks were cooking up had to go someplace. Freddie and Fannie were ready, willing, and very able.

Fannie Mae / Freddie Mac

Just barely getting through the summer of 2008, in the heat of the presidential election season, on Sep. 7, 2008, "Fannie" and "Freddie" were essentially nationalized. They were placed under the conservatorship of the Federal Housing Finance Agency. The U.S. Taxpayer had come to their rescue investing about $200 billion to cover the companies' losses. Obama had yet to be inaugurated. Like all good things, at first. the government experts got it wrong and thought that $100 Billion would be enough and Treasury Secretary Paulson had put a ceiling of $100 billion for investments in each company.

So, again I ask, what does this have to do with President Barack Obama? In February 2009, before completing his first full month of office, with the Obama administration, not wanting to interfere with Bush "blame" inertia, the new Treasury Secretary Tim Geithner raised the ante for Fannie and Freddie to $200 billion. The money was authorized by the Housing and Economic Recovery Act of 2008. Most regular taxpayers figured that was part of the bailout. Ironically, it was a bailout that was "pre-bailout." The big bailout had not yet happened and its money was separate.

First Auto "Bailout" -- Auto Industry 2008

In the pre-bailout category, in late September 2008, Congress was picking at the National Treasury again as it approved a $630 billion plus spending bill. The intent of this bill was to enable spending for "normal" stuff until March 2009, when a new and probably more friendly (to Democrats) President would be in office. The bill included $25 billion in loans to the auto industry at a time when none of the Big Three were whining publicly that they were close to the end. These low-interest loans were intended to aid the industry in its push to build more fuel-efficient, environmentally-friendly vehicles. The Detroit 3 -- General Motors, Ford and Chrysler -- were to be the primary beneficiaries. This one was actually some pork from the democratically controlled congress. The Unions made me do it! Don't ever expect to get this money back.

The Bush transition to Obama occurred during the beginning of what some of us might call the "Great Recession." Let's let the dictionary people define depression. Because the US has gone socialist since the 1920's, there is no question that this terrible economic situation has not affected as many people because of things like Social Security and Medicare. Thus, at least somebody had money to spend.

Troubled Asset Relief Program - TARP

The Emergency Economic Stabilization Act of 2008 (EESA) is commonly referred by taxpayers simply as the first "bailout." In fact, its intent was to bailout the U.S. financial system in response to the subprime mortgage crisis. It gave Congress (Treasury) the right to spend up to $700 billion to purchase toxic, a.k.a. distressed assets such as mortgage-backed securities. Just (ahem!) $350 billion was to be released in 2008 to see how effective the bailout would be and perhaps they would not release the other $350B.

Remember those mortgages that nobody cared about because of the CRA? They were like sharks circling the cove. Everybody knew they were there to bite, and then they did.

The purpose of the EESA bill, of course, was to do other things than merely bail out the dying banks. For example, it was to infuse capital into banks so they had money to loan to stimulate business growth. At first just US banks were the only banks included but then our generous lawmakers modified the bill to enable both foreign and domestic banks to share in the taxpayer funded bailout. How nice!

Even American Express got in on the largesse, right under the wire. The Federal Reserve had just approved its bank-holding application so they got a few bucks also. Over time, the bill grew from three pages to 451 pages. Nobody polled the honorables to see if they had read the bill. It passed as an amendment H.R. 1424 and President Bush signed it on October 3, just a month from the Obama election victory. The cash was supposed to actually become available within two weeks, but you know how government time tables are in reality.

TARP Cash for Obama

Three months after the passing of the resolution and probably more like two months after the cash began to be distributed, President-Elect Obama, Harry Reid, and Nancy Pelosi were blaming George Bush on a regular basis as the perception persisted that the bailout had not worked. They gave it just two months to work before the "Bush did it!" drumbeat began. Yet, Mr. Obama could not say "no" himself to the prospects of giving up $350 billion of taxpayer money that he could dole out. Ironically, because it did not work, Obama needed more.

Because the opportunity was so great, Obama lobbied the majority Democrats for several days in private to get the other $350 billion before its passage on January 15, 2009, just 5 days before his own inauguration. Clearly this half of the $700 billion and the unspent funds from the Bush half are in the Obama column, not the Bush column.

In all government actions, there is irony. In this case, consider that after helping ACORN get the country into the financial mess as ACORN lobbied and protested at banks to make bad loans, Mr. Obama stood ready, even prior to his inauguration to be the instrument to make everything all-right again. It's over a year later and the economy is still in the toilet. None of the 3 million jobs have been created and 3 million more have been lost. Seventeen percent of Americans are out of work as I pen this book. In the blame game, surely there is some Bush residue on some of the cash but the doling out of all this money is right at the feet of Obama?

The then President-elect was tickled pink:

>*"I'm gratified that a majority of the U.S. Senate, both Democrats and Republicans, voted today to give me the authority to implement the rest of the financial rescue plan in a new and responsible way, I know this wasn't an easy vote because of the frustration so many of us share about how the first half of this plan was implemented. There was too little transparency and accountability, and it didn't do enough to get credit where it's needed most -- small businesses and families struggling to keep their jobs and make ends meet."*

This was the mandatory shot at the bad Bush Administration from the all-good and all capable Obama Administration.

>*"Now my pledge is to change the way this plan is implemented and keep faith with the American tax payer by placing strict*

conditions on CEO pay and providing more loans to small businesses, more transparency so that taxpayers can see where their money is spent, and more sensible regulations that will protect consumers, investors, and businesses."

Despite his words, he gave all the money to loyal unions and none whent to help the US infrastructure. He really is a great orator. Here we are about a year later and everything but the stock market is in the toilet and even the Congressional Oversight Panel isn't sure what happened to all the TARP money, or whether the "toxic assets are bought and paid for. Small businesses got no relief. Banks still are not lending to them. Moreover, the job losses are coming from the inability of small businesses to cope with the realities of the economy. Obama had done nothing to make the small business and jobs picture better. Experts cautioned that tax breaks and incentives were required to help small businesses be in a position to start the jobs engine, but no help arrived.

Though he promised transparency, he is more secretive than any President in my lifetime. All work from this White House is a big secret. Moreover, the President has been preoccupied trying to mow over the American people with his single payer healthcare plan destined to bury Americans in more and more debt.

And as an aside, with a wink and a nod he is promising that by cutting $620 billion from Medicare and eliminating Medicare Advantage, he'll be able to provide better healthcare to Seniors. Hah! With all of his emphasis on healthcare, neither he nor the Congress have had any time to observe the economy collapsing under the weight of their ineptness.

Since the beginning, Treasury has been doling out the money via an alphabet soup of different programs, mostly indiscernible to the common American. There is no accounting for $700 billion. The notion is that the banks, the same folks who got us into this mess, with government complicity, can best determine how to use the TARP money the public loans them. That's about the extent of the control.

I don't want to make a mockery of this effort but in many ways it seems it is a friends and family program. Since most of us are not bosom buddies and are not related to Tim Geithner, the embattled Treasury Secretary and his cronies, none of this aid has reached ordinary citizens or small businesses. Here's a little tally of companies getting part of the $700 billion in TARP funds.

- ✓ American International Group (A.I.G.) -- 2008 - 2009
- ✓ CitiGroup 2008
- ✓ Bank of America 2009
- ✓ Over 300 Other Financial Institutions

American International Group (A.I.G.) -- 2008 - 2009

Way back in October, 2008, AIG went on the dole. It was approaching bankruptcy. The Feds had been watching for several months so it was no surprise. Somehow after the Feds let Lehman Brothers fail without the benefit of a bailout, to many it was surprising that when AIG let out its big whimper that it was in big trouble, all of a sudden, AIG could be bailed out and Lehman could fail. Why? The Feds said that AIG was deemed too huge (its assets top $1 trillion), too global and too interconnected to the health of the financial system to fail.

For all these reasons, plus surely a friends and family connection, the government gave AIG an $85 billion loan. Only in the wake of the trillions that we have seen flying out of the treasury for one Obama reason after another, does $85 billion seem small. Ladies and Gentlemen, no matter what the laws of large numbers is telling you, $85 billion is not small.

The financial markets have gotten so complex that the experts do not really know the financial picture of AIG. They do not understand exactly why AIG got its big share of government funds. Remember, Bear Stearns was permitted to fail. Was AIG too big to fail? Nobody had a real clue as to the potential consequences of the impact of AIG's failure on the US and global financial market. Yet, they were so big, that experts feared that their failure could bring about total chaos, whatever that means.

AIG dealt in these instruments called credit-default swaps which they sold in large quantities to just about every financial institution in the world. Because of this, there were some estimates that if AIG was not helped out of its jam, its partners would almost immediately suffer losses in the neighborhood of $180 billion. Yes, $180 billion is a lot of money. Yet AIG is a reckless company that had no more save-worthiness than Lehman Bros or Bear Stearns. They knew that the financial instruments they were buying and selling had a big downside if the price of real estate went down. It did and they were on the verge of collapse before being rescued by your money.

Along the way to today, Americans developed a distaste for AIG. The company became the poster child as the ungrateful servant always on the take but never willing to give. After taking the money to avoid total failure, they somehow acted like they were successful and as most Americans recall, they began to dole out huge bonuses to executives. We document that no less than four times AIG came to the treasury well and the government bailed them out so they did not collapse. Is that management team worthy of a bonus? The ante started with the $85 billion credit line from the Federal Reserve and climbed to a combined $180 billion effort provided from the Treasury ($70 billion) and the Fed ($110 billion). $40 billion of the Treasury's commitment was also included in the TARP total. Yes, that is an awful lot of money to reward a scoundrel.

Even though it's becoming harder and harder to find a reason to like AIG, they do seem to have some major pull with players from both the Bush and Obama Administrations. In July, 2009, the New York Times, a media outlet that has not met a corporation they ever liked, blasted AIG for being liars, cheats, dirty players and deserving of nothing. Many of us felt that intuitively but our representatives chose to give them a few of our bucks from our National Treasury, anyway.

The Times reviewed the state regulatory filings and they found out some interesting things. For example,

> *"AIG's individual insurance companies have been doing an unusual volume of business with each other for many years — investing in each other's stocks; borrowing from each other's investment portfolios; and guaranteeing each other's insurance policies, even when they have lacked the means to make good. Insurance examiners working for the states have occasionally flagged these activities, to little effect."*

> *"More ominously, many of A.I.G.'s insurance companies have reduced their own exposure by sending their risks to other companies, often under the same A.I.G. umbrella".*

So, not only was AIG a bad guy that got bailed out but the AIG risk is so big that our federal regulators have been trying to put a positive spin on AIG's new round of unethical behavior so that they (the regulators) do not put our (taxpayer) stake in AIG at risk. It is a pretty tough day in Peoria when after shelling out billions to make AIG work that we have to walk on eggs to properly regulate it without putting our investment at risk. The AIG debacle makes the Bear Stearns investment look like chump change.

CitiGroup 2008

Citigroup, the huge NY based bank had its hand out for $25 billion investment through the TARP in October and another

$20 billion in November. (That $45 billion is also included in the TARP total.) Additional aid has come in the form of government guarantees to limit losses from a $301 billion pool of toxic assets. In addition to the Treasury's $5 billion commitment, the FDIC has committed $10 billion and the Federal Reserve up to about $220 billion. Fear not, its possibilities add up to just $280 billion. By September 2009, Citigroup owed "just" $50 Billion and it would be nice to think that some of that might come back.

Bank of America 2009

Bank of America picked up a cool $45 billion through the TARP, which included $10 billion originally intended for Merrill Lynch. In addition, the government has made guarantees to limit losses from a $118 billion pool of troubled assets. Additionally, Treasury made a $7.5 billion commitment; the FDIC has committed $2.5 billion and the Federal Reserve is in for up to $87.2 billion.

Some Thought Financial TARP Might Work Out

With the bulk of Americans, most of whom have never been bailed out by the government, howling hard about corporate welfare in the form of the bailouts, it would be minimal consolation if someone really proved that the TARP had earned the taxpayers a ride out of the deficit. However, just like the one and only "cost of living" index is built to take money from the pockets of those who depend on an accurate accounting and put it into the hands of those, such as the oil chieftains, who have gotten more than their fair share, government has a propensity to -- can we say it in this book -- "lie."

What can I mean? I mean that if one company paid back $2 billion in interest to the National Treasury, somebody in the Bush or Obama Administration would be asking why the US is

not investing in more poor, crooked companies. So, when I
show you the rest of the stuff in this Chapter, please note that I
know, and you know, that the NY Times has put the best "spin"
on the information. More than likely none of it is false, but the
whole NY Times article is slanted as if the best thing anybody,
including taxpayer funded agencies, can do is invest in those
who are about to go out of business. If that sounds silly, it sure
ought to.

Right now, the New York Times may even admit that there is
more risk than reward in the TARP packages, if you are the
government, hiding under the name, "taxpayers," Hey, taxpayers
are still on the hook. But, because all banks do not have death
wishes, and maybe because ACORN is being watched very
closely on multiple fronts, a number of smart banks are not
taking bad risk loans. Much to the chagrin of those who passed
out the bailout dollars, these banks, practicing an almost
forgotten notion once known a fiscal responsibility, are slowly
recovering, or so it seems.

Of course Bank of America and CitiGroup, described above, are
the ones with most risk. These two biggies have not made any
return yet and thus, there is the potential that there may be a big
loss. And for the skeptics out there, who knows what Freddie
and Fannie are doing!

By September, 2009, the US Government was reporting on most
of the good news on its TARP "investments. The New York
Times was so thrilled with the news that they immediately
declared that all who were not working should feel as good as if
they were working. OK, I gave myself up on the NYT, but the
NYT reporting on this is almost as good as the great tingling of
MSNBC correspondent Chris Matthews' leg during the Obama
campaign. And, yes, these few comments give strong indication
that I did see the Obama love-in healthcare speech to Congress
on September 9, 2009, but I am hiding behind words to assure I
am not called out. Can you imagine that?

Anyway, near the middle of September, 2009, the NY Times begged that the U.S. government was starting to see profits from the $700 billion Troubled Asset Relief Program (TARP), started last year to thwart the financial crisis. However, they acknowledged that the two largest recipients of TARP money - Citigroup Inc. and Bank of America Corp. have yet to pay back dime one of their loans and the government (taxpayers in this case) are still exposed to possible losses from these two heavyweights. Oh, and they also noted that there are also a number of smaller U.S. banks that may not bring in the bacon as promised.

So far, however, according to the midnight calculations of the NY Times, and their special billion dollar tingling rounding machines, the government has picked up about $4 billion - the NYT equivalent of a 15% annual return - from eight of the biggest banks that have fully repaid their loans to Uncle Sam. Of course the debt is in the trillions, but who is counting? The partial list of the biggies is as follows:

- ✓ Goldman Sachs Group Inc. --> $1.4 billion in profit.
- ✓ Morgan Stanley --> $1.3 billion in profit.
- ✓ American Express Co. --> $414 million in profit.
- ✓ Five other banks = Northern Trust Corp. , The Bank of New York Mellon Corp., State Street Corp., U.S. Bancorp (NYSE: USB), and BB&T Corp. --> between $100 million and $334 million
- ✓ Fourteen smaller banks --> $35 million in profit.

Not accounted for at the time of the NYT analysis, JPMorgan Chase & Co. and Capital One Financial Corp. were expected to yield an additional profit of more than $3.1 billion, according to the Times.

There's Trouble in Paradise:

As tough as it is to believe in the day and age of one major billion dollar mistake after another, the government has an oversight panel. It is called the Congressional Oversight Panel (COP) and recently they said that "It is likely that an overwhelming portion of the troubled assets from last October remain on bank balance sheets today." Yes, you heard it right. We are now about a year into TARP, which was not designed to bolster bank profits but to relieve the system of toxic assets / troubled assets, and yet they continue to be a substantial danger to the financial system. Somebody missed something someplace.

The COP report continued:

> *"If the economy worsens, especially if unemployment remains elevated or if the commercial real estate market collapses, then defaults will rise and the troubled assets will continue to deteriorate in value. Banks will incur further losses on their troubled assets. The financial system will remain vulnerable to the crisis conditions that TARP was meant to fix."*

So, it appears that the $700 billion bailout designed to solve a problem caused by a major mismanagement of the financial system by the government, has been mismanaged. Please tell me why anybody would want to place the whole of healthcare into a management team such as the Federal Government. There is a flip saying about the lack of ability of some to manage. It goes like this, "they could screw up a one car funeral," which may belittle graphic, but to the point. Place these managers in front of healthcare and I think we can expect them to cause quite a few more funerals than we have today.

Chapter 4 Sin 2 of 7. Indoctrination of American Children

Is Obama a Communist?

As we all know, some of the big jabs that come at President Obama are a result of his image as a Messiah to many of his worshippers. I could have said followers, but those who call Obama the "Anointed One" and the Messiah and such would suggest that it is more than just a following. It is a mass of adoring worshippers. To an extent, they are right. In my lifetime, other than JFK, who never capitalized on it in public, I have never seen a President with such rock-star status, presence and acceptance. Even in his waning years in 2016, he still gets the great looks and the accolades. "When will they ever learn?"

I am not the only one who sees it that way. I am not a worshipper or a follower of the President. I watch him with a wary eye. Entertainment Weekly is both a follower, and as their stories show, deep worshippers also. On the Web severl years ago, they had this to say about this special President: "He's bigger than Brangelina, bigger than Beyonce: See how our new president has become the biggest celebrity in the world, and is changing pop culture forever."

I probably should not be writing this section, because I did not recognize any names in the EW quote. I don't mean that I did not know the two people referred, to I mean I had not seen any names in the quote -- "Brangelina" and "Beyonce" -- you gotta be kidding me.

As hard as it may be for some to believe, there are a few out here who are not only "non-followers," they actually do not like the man. Others do not like what he is doing. Many of the nastiest blogs on the right side of the political fence paint Obama out as a downright card carrying communist. Some suggest that he is more like the National Socialists (Nazis) in Germany.

I am not sure of the former; but, from what I see, he is nothing like the latter. I can stop that thought right now in its tracks before we proceed any further in this chapter. From my own observations, and I have many observations in many venues of our semi-new President, he does not appear to have any nationalist tendencies.

He is not strumming up allegiance for America at every stop. There is no apparent undying love for America and its traditions. You have to be in love with a country (nationalist) as a prerequisite to be a Nazi. He is not a Nazi. I am pretty sure of that.

To David Axelrod and Rahm Emanuel, now Mayor of Chicago, the above comments might be strong enough to be called out by the Thought Police, but my comments are actually a compliment, compared to the bloggers to whom I alluded above. The fact that he did not sing God Bless America at every campaign stop, is proof superior that President Obama is definitely not a Nazi.

Nationalist Socialism is designed to get people excited about their country and it is billed as being good for a country. This would ultimately reflect back upon its leader as such love for country would be engendered by the leader. It's not that our leader would mind having positive reflection coming back at him. His ego is huge enough that it would soak it all up sooner than a professional tanner could soak up a day of sun. But he does not appear ready to share the spotlight with his country. So, we should not have to worry about Nazism. Communism, progressivism, and socialism, perhaps, but not NAZISM. The president does not seem to like America enough to be an American Nazi.

We can rule out fascism, on the same grounds as Nazism, as there is no great love for the home turf. Just as Nazism, the central theme of fascism is the state, the government of the home country. The state is supreme and everything revolves around the state in a fascist country. So, the Nazis were fascists, but the fascists were not necessarily Nazis. The Nazis were racists in that their anti-Semitic notions guided them as much as their love for their homeland. The verdict is that Barack Hussein Obama is not a fascist. I hope that makes Axelrod and Emanuel (Rahm) happy.

Obama's people and Obama himself have never cried out when he was declared a "progressive." So, of all other things that he may be, Obama and company appear to tacitly acknowledge that he is a progressive. He and they do not mind when he is accused of adopting socialist principles as they are benign and benevolent and apparently for the people, but they might not agree that he is a socialist.

Karl Marx had great disdain for the owners of capital. He felt the owners had too much and theirs should be taken and divvied up among the workers and then, who-the-hell-cared what happened to the owners. Surely, the workers could not get the owners' share without some hurting or dead owners left on the countryside. And, so if Marxism is implemented, there may be calls for violence to achieve its simple objectives. We're talking about somebody losing their land and property and factories perhaps and somebody else getting it. You don't think that would be bloodless? What would you do if all of a sudden somebody said that your house was going to be given to another family who needed it more than you?

Communists believe that the state should control everything, including industry. So, in this scenario, out of nowhere, the government begins to control huge segments of society, such as the automobile industry, the financial industry, and the healthcare industry. Did I just say that? Is that happening here?

Barack Hussein Obama is clearly for two things: 1. Redistribution of income, and 2. Redistribution of healthcare benefits. Much truth is said in jest. The latter, said in jest, is just a more specific instance of the former. If you believe in redistribution of income, it can be argued that you are a socialist as the confiscated income will help the masses.

It can also be argued that the President is a Marxist, as Marx had such a negative notion of the owner class since "the rich get richer and the poor get poorer." Marx tried to figure out a way to evaluate a worker's contribution to society and was extremely annoyed that the labor of the masses resulted in the affluent becoming more affluent. Other than wanting to maintain his own affluence, it seems that President Obama fits the mold of, at a minimum, a closet Marxist.

Have we returned to "Is Obama a Communist?" already? We all know from late grade school or early high school that communism with a small "c" is the ideology summarized by that "who-can-say-no-to-that" maxim, "From each according to his ability, to each according to his need." Of course, there is always the problem of whose hand it is that is going to distribute what, from whom, to whom. Arguments resulting in death have occurred, over time, for lesser reasons.

Let's suppose an elephant is going to be examined by a group of blind people, as was told in an old Indian story I found on the Web. If our understanding of communism were to be formed based on the perceptions of these blind men, it would vary greatly depending on which portion of the animal they touched. Communism with a small c is easy to define. It is the whole deal for the masses. When we think of "communism," we can see it as that huge elephant in the jungle with all those strange parts, working together as a whole. Contrast that with Communism with a capital "C" as perhaps just an elephant tusk – perceived, by its fearful examiner, as a sharp and dangerous spear. What "C"ommunist country of which you are aware does not have a violent history?

Karl Marx and Fredrich Engels were economists. Tim Geithner is an economist. Now you know why there was a problem with communism. They tried to answer the puzzle of the day: why are the poor, poor and the rich, rich? Marx and Engels published the Communist Manifesto," in 1848, to answer this question, for eternity. Their interpretations sent men to their graves, for eternity, far sooner than if the two had been quiet. They declared that many problems in society occur because of unequal distribution of wealth. Have you heard that recently in the U.S.? They were convinced that happiness and prosperity for all would occur if the distinctions between the rich and poor of society were eliminated. Think about the only ways that can be achieved -- a highly aggressive tax policy or a revolution.
.

Marx and Engels were not necessarily prayerful men and so God chose not to intervene. They knew that without God's intervention, which they expected would never happen, the rich would never give up their goods or status voluntarily. Thus, a rebellion of the poor, which they liked to suggest were the "working class," in their class system, would be necessary. As economists, neither was gun wielding, yet they had to know that such a transfer of wealth would never occur without bloodshed. This philosophy, known as Marxism, was perceived by many as the cure for the rich owning too much. As such, it was the major underpinning of communism.

So, is Obama a communist? I have no idea. He is scary in his notions of redistribution of wealth, however. We'll let the historians figure the answer to that ultimate question. But, a word to the wise for Mr. Obama. If you don't want the world to think you are a communist, it would help if you chose not to take over any more industries.

What is Indoctrination?

The big Obama sin of indoctrination came about as Americans were sending their kids back to school for the start of the school year in the fall 2009. The Obama administration put together some material and the President addressed the children. Alarms were raised throughout the country as many Americans saw this as indoctrination in a similar vein as one might find it in a Communist country.

Freedictionary.com defines indoctrination in these two ways:

1. To instruct in a body of doctrine or principles.
2. To imbue with a partisan or ideological point of view: a generation of children who had been indoctrinated against the values of their parents.

It was the second hit on a Google search.

There are many Americans who, after a year of Obama, believe he does not represent their thoughts. They were not necessarily sure at first but over time, they made the decision. Never has so much controversial legislation been rammed through an American public. Because of his actions and his speeches, there is much open discussion about whether or not the President supports an ideology like one of the "isms" above.

Because nobody is really sure, people who otherwise would not care are watching the President like a hawk. According to history, the socialist movements across the world all started off gently to help the poor using funding from the rich, but communist activities quickly merged into maniacal movements in which neither the poor nor the rich benefited. The only winners were those in the resulting government.

Does Obama Think Like You Do?

As much as everybody loves the First Lady, few have forgotten that Michelle Obama was not necessarily happy with America, until her husband became President. All the time that her husband, Barack Hussein Obama, has been President, he has done more apologizing for "bad America" to far too many people than many Americans can stomach.

In some ways, it seems that he is suggesting that the Richard Prior and Gene Wilder notion of America as "We's bad!" is actually true. Rather than tell the world that the "bad" notion is way false, and that America is a great country and Americans are a great people, he consistently chooses the low road and apologizes at the drop of a hat. Thus, he has gained worldwide esteem for himself while denigrating the USA and the American people.

It is as if we are all schlocks and that gets old! The bottom line is that many Americans are concerned about who this great campaigner actually is in person, and why is he so ashamed of us that he's constantly apologizing?. Should this apologetic, socialist-leaning, progressive-behaving, potentially otherwise good, man be giving advice to the children of people who unequivocally love America? That's it in a nutshell! Sorry!

So now, why were the critics on the right decrying Obama's welcome back to school message for all the kids in America? Hey, he is the President! The bottom line is that if they trusted him when they voted for him, as many did, that same good will does not exist anymore. Obama burned his capital with his seven deadly programs. Americans were alive through 2009, watching events that they could not believe unfold before their very eyes. Many people began to lose that trust. It's that simple.

They then questioned whether they wanted "this guy," to speak to their kids. They were no longer completely sure about him and even though they were hopeful for the next three years, they would not have chosen Obama to deliver the official message of back-to-school in America to their kids. In fact, those least in favor labeled the whole idea, "Obama's Indoctrination Plan for Students."

You may all recall September 2009, when there was even a suggested lesson plan that called for students to write letters to themselves about how they could help President Obama accomplish his agenda. By September, with all the unread legislation that had passed, there were many who no longer trusted what they now saw as the "superintendent in chief." Nobody was interested in having to tell their kids that Obama is a so and so or a such and such when the kids come home thinking that maybe even the Lord is not as powerful as mmm mmm mm Barack Hussein Obama.

The more people rationally tried to digest this Obamspeak, hearing the Whitehouse worshippers say that the speech was merely "designed to encourage kids to stay in school," did not help matters one bit. The idea of kids being indoctrinated into the world of Obama really was at the basis of the whole controversy. Though some pointed out that Reagan and Bush and others had done the same thing, with Democrats objecting to high heaven, I might add, none of the other Presidents gave reason for concern that the lesson from instructor-in-chief might be a reading from the Communist Manifesto or Das Kapital.

On the Media Matters Web site (www.mediamatters.com), they wanted to show that conservatives were wacky when they thought that the President had any other intentions, but were concerned about what would be best for the children. So, they posted what they thought were outlandish perspectives and permitted liberal bloggers to comment. http://mediamatters.org/research/200909020012

> *"Numerous conservatives have claimed that President Obama's upcoming September 8 speech about "persisting and succeeding in school," along with classroom activities about the "importance of education," will "indoctrinate" and "brainwash" schoolchildren. Conservatives have compared Obama's address to Chinese communism and the Hitler Youth, while also calling for parents to "keep your kids home" from the "fascist in chief."*

Nobody is calling Obama out as Hitler or Mao, but it is a fact that forced praise and participation of one's agenda and mission is called indoctrination. Sorry "Media Matters," you don't really matter in this discussion.

There were many who were not as trusting as the liberal press, who felt this should be stopped. Frederick Hess, for example, Director of Education Policy Studies at the American Enterprise Institute, which is a conservative think tank, said the suggested lesson plans cross the line between instruction and advocacy. His specific words to describe how he saw it are as follows:

> *"I don't think it's appropriate for teachers to ask students to help promote the president's preferred school reforms and policies. It very much starts to set up the president as a superintendent in chief. ... There's a lot of people on both sides of the political spectrum who will rightfully be concerned with the president's call to action."*

After reading the Department of Education lesson plans for the speech, Neal McCluskey, who is an Associate Director of Cato Institute's Center for Educational Freedom, noted, impartially, that there were things that would clearly set off "alarm bells," for Americans including a style and language that attempts to "glorify President Obama" in the minds of young students. From McCluskey's point of view, it was a "blatantly political move, nobody knows for sure, but it gives that impression. You don't want to see this coming from the President, You don't want to see this coming from the federal government."

Obamaday came and went, without incident, as the feds released the obviously toned down message so late in the game. They could have avoided a lot of angst if they had released the text sooner, but maybe the text was completely rewritten. That is what the skeptics think, and the vigilance will continue, so that the kids cannot be used as pawns to project any politician's agenda.

Mmm Mmm Mm

A few weeks later in September, some teachers, who had not gotten the message that Obama had resigned as the superintendent in chief, trained their school children to be able to sing very complimentary songs lauding the President. The irony is that in one song, which had originally been about Jesus Christ, instead of the term "Jesus Christ," the words "Barack Hussein Obama" were inserted, giving messianic qualities to the President in this education setting.

The tune from "Jesus Loves the Little Children of the World was modified other than one verse which was too good to resist. If the original was sung, the teachers and all the students would have been arrested for practicing religion in school. Since Obama-worship is not yet recognized as a religion, all were saved and none have had to do time in the Big House.

The kids were singing songs that were seemingly overflowing with campaign slogans and praise for "Barack Hussein Obama." The little ones repeatedly chanted the president's name and celebrated all his wonderful accomplishments, some equal to those of Jesus, including Obama's "great plans" to "make this country's economy Number 1 again."

Here is the song. What do you think?

> Mmm, mmm, mm!
> Barack Hussein Obama
>
> He said that all must lend a hand
> To make this country strong again
> Mmm, mmm, mm!
> Barack Hussein Obama
>
> He said we must be fair today
> Equal work means equal pay
> Mmm, mmm, mm!
> Barack Hussein Obama

He said that we must take a stand
To make sure everyone gets a chance
Mmm, mmm, mm!
Barack Hussein Obama

He said red, yellow, black or white
All are equal in his sight
Mmm, mmm, mm!
Barack Hussein Obama

Now, let's contrast this with the song from which the major line comes. Do you think if Jesus were President, this would have played well in Washington?

Jesus loves the little children
All the children of the world
Black and yellow, red and white
They're all precious in His sight
Jesus loves the little children of the world

Whether you're rich or whether you're poor
It matters not to Him
He remembers where you're going
Not where you've been

Jesus loves the little children
All the children of the world
Black and yellow, red and white
They're all precious in His sight
Jesus loves the little children of the world

If your heart is troubled
Don't worry, don't you fret
He knows that you have heard His call
And he won't forget

Jesus loves the little children
All the children of the world
Black and yellow, red and white
They're all precious in His sight
Jesus loves the little children of the world

All around the world tonight
His children rest assured
That He will watch and He will keep us
Safe and secure

Jesus loves the little children
All the children of the world
Black and yellow, red and white
They're all precious in His sight
Jesus loves the little children of the world

Thanks to http://www.kididdles.com/lyrics/j007.html.

There are people who go nuts when anybody compares anybody, other than Ahmed Ahmadinejad, with Adolph Hitler. I am not and I repeat, I am not making a comparison of Barack Obama and Adolph Hitler. This chapter is about the powerful role youth indoctrination can have on a country. Germany, in the late 1920s through the war, was a powerful example of a country gone astray and youth indoctrination had a major role.

Few hold the happenings in Germany, at this time in history, in any high regard. Adolph Hitler was the master at youth indoctrination and it paid off big for him, but not for Germany. Look at the little innocent song above, followed by the Jesus version from which its theme was extracted. Now, let me ask you if the next song / prayer brings to you the same sense of innocence.

http://www.spartacus.schoolnet.co.uk/GERyouth.htm

Baldur von Schirach, the head of the Hitler Youth (HJ) wrote a prayer that had to be said by members of the Hitler Youth before meals.

> Fuehrer, my Fuehrer given me by God,
> Protect and preserve my life for long.
> You rescued Germany from its deepest need.
> I thank you for my daily bread.
> Stay for a long time with me, leave me not.
> Fuehrer, my Fuehrer, my faith, my light
> Hail my Fuehrer.

In 1936, Baldur von Schirach wrote a poem about Adolf Hitler that members of the Hitler Youth had to memorize and recite.

> That is the greatest thing about him,
> That he is not only our leader and a great hero,
> But himself, upright, firm and simple,
> In him the roots of our world.
> And his soul touches the stars
> And yet he remains a man like you and me.

I know that is sick but facts are facts. If it were not Adolph Hitler that the youth prayed to/ for, this might appear to be very innocent, but it was clearly indoctrination. That is why there is extreme sensitivity to a President who does not have the full trust of his people, messing around with the thoughts of American children. All one needs to do is mention the proverbial "slippery slope" and the lawyers get the message immediately.

So, Big Deal???

Nobody is suggesting that Barack Hussein Obama is trying to rule the world by taking over the minds of little children or even those children a bit older. Even more than the fantasies of George Bush, however, many have concluded that Obama would actually like to rule the world. Some see it as his "rightful" place. T

herefore, all these little notions about how to achieve lifetime rule in your own country have some play in the discussion. When I grew up, no kids even cared about the rest of the world because America was the beacon of hope. Some think that President Obama would be happy if that beacon went out and another one, that he would build, could be ignited in his stead. Therefore, parents must take care of their children, no matter who may be the President.

FrontPageMagazine.com's David Yeagley knows that communism needs children.

> *It is only children who will obey the tyranny of adult delusions without question. Yeagley says that "only the young are naïve enough to hate all authority and to destroy all achievement. For youth, Communism is not a delusion, but an exciting, heroic cause."*

Tyrants the world over have loved existing while the children grew to be adults. If you could get them before they were thinking for themselves, then you had them forever. Even in the Vietnam War, the infamous Pol Pot, from Cambodia, knew the power of the young. He overtook his country way back in April 1975.

What did he use to be successful? Those like me, alive back then, know of a gang called the Khmer Rouge (Killing Fields). Using these teens, Pol Pot was able to murder nearly 2 million people in his own nation, close to 1/3 of all the people in the country.

With the "kids" on his side, he did it in less than four years. Communism was the mantra, but somebody always leads and those with a will and a mind to resist are not tolerated. Cambodia's Pol Pot created a society of pure Communism. It was as bad as it gets -- ghastly, murderous, and tyrannical.

Communism, they say, is the god of discontent. It needs no blessing. All it needs is a people in need and "soldiers" of the people with hearts willing to hate, and as some would say, willing to call envy "justice." It is the upside down of right side up. There can be no equality other than the violent destruction of all social and cultural distinctions that once kept people from harmful acts of violence. Freedom, in this environment, means you have signed up to permit absolute dictatorship over the people, and as Rod Serling might say, you do not realize that it is you who is not free.

Communication -- Not a Friend of Communists

A Communist dictatorship becomes possible for a number of reasons, but it is sustained by indoctrination. If you miss the children, you miss the game. The word for controlling the youth is "communications." A lot of people have acted like they felt people were over-reacting to the Obama speech to apparently take over the school children across the nation. Why would parents not want their children to hear the most gifted speaker since Bill Clinton, the master of eloquence?

I think we can net it out immediately by being honest. We'll say it again. People did not and do not trust Obama, even as much (or little) as Bill Clinton. The people were concerned about what he would say to their children. Reading from the annals of history and exploring the potentialities of the "isms," the stakes are very high. Still, there is another problem in that, over time, there has been a pattern of major indoctrination-type situations with school children that came into play, often before bad things happened. One of those is eerily reminiscent of 1930's Germany.

Please do not shut this book down if we mention Adolph Hitler. Nobody is suggesting that Barack Hussein Obama and Adolph Hitler have anything in common. Those sensitive to indoctrination are concerned about powerful government leaders giving children the "right" message. If we look at history we can see that it does not take too long for the "right message" to be the "only message." Worse than that, for youth indoctrination, it is just a little while later that the government wants to speak to the children directly, without parental influence. Nobody thinks we are going there, but due caution has been raised. Since it has been raised, we discuss Hitler in the context of mobilizing the youth for his diabolical purposes.

Clearly the Hitler notion could not be resisted in its day, as even our Pope Benedict, a kind and wonderful man, was lured into the Hitler Youth Movement. The fact is that, back then, you were either in or you were dead.

Hitler Was a Good Ole Boy

Hitler actually started with a local grass roots notion. They gradually gained a huge following and over time they felt that they could begin bullying and strong arming those who were not like minded. Eventually they were "forced" to silence people who did not agree with them. Silencing meant either a re-indoctrination or a few days of mourning for a specific family. Eventually, as people disappeared and then there were funerals, the regular people stopped confronting the Nazis and resorted to quietly grumbling rather than being eliminated. Normal human beings would have never thought what happened would happen or even could happen.

Hitler gradually built up his following and as noted, he made his enemies disappear. Sound familiar? That is another reason why the conservative media in the US today is very concerned about the Obama enemies list. Things went along and most people just kept going about their daily lives, not paying much attention to politics. Yet wherever they went, morning, noon and night, there was this loud-mouthed Austrian, not even a German by birth, with a chip on his shoulder telling all the people how they would now lead their lives.

Nobody ever suggested that Hitler was not eloquent in his speeches. He was the best speaker there ever was. He spoke often and loudly. He did not tell the people anything about his real intentions or he would have been long gone. He told them he was going to "change" Germany to its former glory. He was the grand simpatico. He was the sin eater. He promised to take all their troubles and wipe them away. People got really excited about that. They wanted hope and they wanted change. Hitler was a 1920's Rock Star.

Eventually and according to plan, people started swearing allegiance to him rather than to the country. The entire nation began to revolve around a Rock Star of a man -- Hitler. His big shtick was to get the Germans hooked while they knew nothing else. He loved the idea of indoctrinating the youth because they stayed his. It all started in real schools and it was innocent or so it seemed.

School children were taught songs praising Hitler and eventually they were required to participate in his youth corp. Back then, they called them Hitler Youth. People with knowledge of history and the power of indoctrination want their children far away from a President who insists on talking to the children.

And, so the "Anointed One" found great resistance in his first attempt to address the children of America without prior parental approval. This is still America. Knowing history, the people saw this as going way beyond teaching children to love their country and respect the President. They saw the Obama intrusion into the classroom a bit Hitler-esque in style and into the realm of indoctrination by elevating the President into a cult like figure.

In the Hitler period, the youth were well subjugated. They were originally like the Boy Scouts. In fact, Germany, during this period, would not permit the Boy Scouts themselves to exist, as it would go against their ultimate youth agenda. The Hitler Youth were all trained to be highly physically fit and it did not matter if they were good or bad students as long as they were strong and they loved the main man. They were viewed as future "Aryan supermen" and were indoctrinated in pro-Hitlerism and anti-Semitism. Their personhood mattered only to themselves, but they never had a chance to think about that.

Indoctrinating children in National Socialist (NAZI) ideology was a key goal of the NAZI Party. The Hitler Youth was not just a German version of the Boy Scouts. The Hitler Youth was more similar to the Soviet Young Pioneers, but even with the Pioneers, there were major differences. From the beginning, Hitler saw the Hitler Youth movement as a tool to hardening boys for their future role of soldiers. He wanted a generation of "victorious active, daring youth, immune to pain." There was to be no "intellectual" training for the boys of the New Order as Hitler viewed intellectual pursuits as damaging to German youth.

Hitler loved the NAZI youth movement, as it was very important to his long term goals. . Hitler was a phenomenally astute politician. He wanted big time power more than one can imagine. Unfortunately, for the German people, he was smart. He knew it would be difficult to seize power and he knew that he would never be able to convert many Germans to National Socialism (Nazi). The younger generation was easy to move to his way of thinking. He exploited that. They willingly came to the Hitler Youth as their classmates had because it was "cool." http://histclo.com/Youth/youth/org/nat/hitler/hitler.htm

From the USHMM United States Holocaust Memorial Museum http://www.ushmm.org/propaganda/themes/indoctrinating-youth/

Shaping the Future: Indoctrinating Youth

> *"These boys and girls enter our organizations [at] ten years of age, and often for the first time get a little fresh air; after four years of the Young Folk they go on to the Hitler Youth, where we have them for another four years . . . And even if they are still not complete National Socialists, they go to Labor Service and are smoothed out there for another six, seven months . . . And whatever class consciousness or social status might still be left . . . the Wehrmacht [armed forces] will take care of that."*
> *-Adolf Hitler, 1938*

During the years 1922-1945, a "Hitler Youth" movement was created. The nature and purpose of the "Hitler Youth movement" included many reasons. It allowed Hitler to have high popularity with young people because they were Germany's future. This would, theoretically, play a vital role in a better Germany.

This idea gained Hitler a chance for naive children to follow his command. Hitler's objective was to introduce young boys to a soldier's life so that one day they would fight to protect their country. This then would give him more power. The youth movement for girls put them in their place and presented to them what was expected of them as young woman. Their destiny was to be the future mothers of important pure bred Germans.

Another purpose of the youth movement was to keep track of what the peers of young children thought of this new government's policies. The Nazis would persuade the members of the group to tell them whether their parents spoke highly of Hitler or not. If not, their parents would be arrested and sent away for "re-education." Movements were set up also to raise money for Nazi charity. Young boys or girls would be sent to collect money from the public for the military's needs.

Joining the Hitler youth movement gave youngsters opportunities to go away on holidays to harden their character by having their physical and mental strength disciplined and improved. In these trips, the youth were also brainwashed to make it easier for them to obey their government.

From the 1920s onwards, the Nazi Party targeted German youth as a special audience for its propaganda messages. These messages emphasized that the Party was a movement of youth: dynamic, resilient, forward-looking, and hopeful. Millions of German young people were won over to Nazism in the classroom and through extracurricular activities

Source for much of the below information: http://www.spartacus.schoolnet.co.uk/GERyouth.htm

Blacks Welcome?

Some of the stories of the Hitler Youth program are all-telling: For example, Hans Massaquoi was born in Germany in 1926. His mom was German, but his dad came from Africa. When he was interviewed by Studs Terkel about his experiences during Nazi Germany for his book, <u>The Good War</u> (1985), he offered this compelling story

> *"There was a drive to enroll young kids into the Hitler Youth movement. I wanted to join, of course. My mother took me aside and said, "Look, Hans, you may not understand, but they don't want you." I couldn't understand. All my friends had these black shorts and brown shirts and a swastika and a little dagger which said Blood and Honor. I wanted it just like everybody else. I wanted to belong. These were my schoolmates.*

> *In 1936, our class had a chance to go to Berlin to watch the Olympics. Not all Germans were sold on this Hitler nonsense. Jesse Owens was the undisputed hero of the German people. He*

was the darling of the 1936 Olympic Games. With the exception of a small Nazi elite, they opened their hearts to this black man who ran his butt off. I was so proud, sitting there.

It's clear to me that had the Nazi leadership known of my existence, I would have ended in a gas oven or at Auschwitz. What saved me was there was no black population in Germany. There was no apparatus set up to catch blacks. The apparatus that was set up to apprehend Jews entailed questionnaires that were mailed to all German households. The question was: Jewish or non-Jewish? I could always, without perjuring myself, write: non-Jewish. http://www.spartacus.schoolnet.co.uk/GERyouth.ht m "

Quotes from the Times

A Schoolteacher wrote a short letter to a friend in December, 1938

In the schools it is not the teacher, but the pupils, who exercise authority. Party functionaries train their children to be spies and agent provocateurs. The youth organizations, particularly the Hitler Youth, have been accorded powers of control which enable every boy and girl to exercise authority backed up by threats. Children have been deliberately taken away from parents who refused to acknowledge their belief in National Socialism. The refusal of parents to "allow their children to join the youth organization" is regarded as an adequate reason for taking the children away.
http://www.spartacus.schoolnet.co.uk/GERyouth.htm

Isle McKee, a young lady, was a member of the German Girls' League, later she recalled her experiences in her autobiography.

We were told from a very early age to prepare for motherhood, as the mother in the eyes of our beloved leader and the National Socialist Government [NAZI] was the most important person in the nation. We were Germany's hope in the future, and it was our duty to breed and rear the new generation of sons and daughter. These lessons soon bore fruit in the shape of quite a few illegitimate small sons and daughters for the Reich, brought forth by teenage members of the League of German Maidens. The girls felt they had done their duty and seemed remarkably unconcerned about the scandal.
http://www.spartacus.schoolnet.co.uk/GERyouth.htm

Jutta Rudiger, who was the head of the German Girls' League, was shocked when she heard a speech given by in 1939 Heinrich Himmler in 1939.

"He said that in the war a lot of men would be killed and therefore the nation needed more children, and it wouldn't be such a bad idea if a man, in addition to his wife, had a girlfriend would bear his children. And I must say, all my leaders were sitting there with their hair standing on end."
http://www.spartacus.schoolnet.co.uk/GERyouth.htm

How about this chilling statement issued by the German government on May 3, 1941?

"The Hitlerjugend (HJ) [Hitler Youth] come to you today with the question: why are you still outside the ranks of the HJ? We take it that you accept your Fuehrer, Adolf Hitler. But you can only do this if you also accept the HJ created by him. If you are for the Fuehrer, therefore for the HJ, then sign the enclosed application. If you are not willing to join the HJ, then write us that on the enclosed blank."
http://www.spartacus.schoolnet.co.uk/GERyouth.htm

How many do you think declined on the enclosed blank? What do you suppose happened to them?

Boys and Girls -- Nazi Youth Movements

Nazi youth leader Baldur von Schirach set up a youth group called the Jungvolk (young people -- youth). It was for boys aged between 10 and 14. It was their entrance into the Nazi mold. It was a far more serious form of our own boy scouts in which the youth were forced to learn things that would help them as they moved up to serve the Reich.

The boys learned semaphore (a means of sending codes with two flags), arms drill, and they took part in multiple day cross-country hikes. Of course, they also learned the Nazi dogma, and eventually were anointed as loyal supporters. Though not compulsory, it might as well have been. In 1936, membership of the Hitler Youth was made compulsory for all boys aged 15 and 18. At the same time, all other youth organizations were banned.

The Nazis had a role for girls and young women also. Young girls from the age of ten onward were taken into organizations where they were taught only two things: to take care of their bodies so they could bear as many children as the state needed and to be loyal to National Socialism.

The Bund Deutscher Mädel (German Girls' League) was the female counterpart of the Hitler Youth. Up to the age of fourteen, girls were known as Young Girls (Jungmädel) and from seventeen to twenty-one they formed a special voluntary organization called Faith and Beauty (Glaube und Schonheit).

"The degree of parental supervision naturally diminished as young people went to camp and hostels for long periods of time. In 1936, when approximately 100,000 members of the Hitler Youth and the Girls' League attended the Nuremberg Rally,

900 girls between fifteen and eighteen returned home pregnant."
http://www.spartacus.schoolnet.co.uk/GERyouth.htm

More babies ultimately meant more Germans!

Red Flag Communism

If you'll pardon the pun, whenever I hear of communism as being accepted in any way as a good idea, a red flag comes up in my mind. It isn't that I don't see some value in a system that sets all people at mediocre and does not permit them to improve. It is probably good for the mediocre and those who are less than mediocre and it makes everybody feel good because nobody is permitted to be superior or excellent. It is not the world in which I would choose to live. I would prefer to be in the lowest class hoping for an opportunity to advance than be in the class of mediocrity, lowered even further to accommodate all people.

Until this current Administration, I never dreamed that there could be so many Marxists in high places in our government. One might conclude that someone was setting us up for a takeover. States (countries such as the US) can evolve to communism or there can be a revolt. Revolution can be slow and methodical, as in Germany, or it can be a big bang like in Russia. Van Jones is a communist and his beliefs were never criticized by the President after the "Green Czar" stepped down. That says something, I think, but the signals are never clear.

We can gain at least some insight into the notion of communism from the master Vladimir Lenin of Russia. We can also get a look at Lenin's character by reading this short monolog that the writer Maxim Gorky reported, of Lenin as a classical music critic:

"I know nothing that is greater than the Appassionata [by Beethoven]; I'd like to listen to it every day [Lenin said]. It is marvelous superhuman music. I always think with pride--

perhaps it is naive of me--what marvelous things human beings can do!

But I can't listen to music too often. It affects your nerves, makes you want to say stupid nice things, and stroke the heads of people who could create such beauty while living in this vile hell. And now you must not stroke anyone's head: you might get your hand bitten off. You have to hit them on the head, without any mercy, although our ideal is not to use force against anyone. Hm, hm, our duty is infernally hard."

mmm mmm mm!

UC Berkeley has some great material on the roots of communism and all the other isms at http://econ161.berkeley.edu/tceh/Slouch_Alternatives12.html. The following quote from this site is spooky, as it has to do with thought.

"As the German Marxist Rosa Luxemburg had warned, the process begins by ruling in the name of the people, then by substituting the judgment of the Party for the wishes of the people, then by substituting the decisions of the Central Committee for the judgment of the Party, and then by substituting the whim of the Dictator for the decisions of the Central Committee."

Is Obama Cause for Concern?

The real question then in 2009, of course, was, "Is Obama Cause for Concern?" I did not think there was a clear answer then. In 2016, he is the most feared ideologue in the US. He is a major progressive, but something more of an ideologue that is anti-American. Progressive is simply a euphemism for someone who believes that the state has all power and individuals receive their power from the state. Can we recover from this guy?

He is a socialist / Marxist in that he believes in redistribution of income, healthcare, energy or whatever else others may have. Thus, he is not a capitalist, and does not ascribe to many American principles. He actually in 2009 was exhibiting disdain for democracy and individual liberty.

Because of the big uproar over Obama indoctrination in early September 2009, the White House Department of Education re-wrote its instructional sheets and restructured its talking points. All of this material was distributed to schools, at great cost, to have the President tell the students to stay in school. It is easy to see that Americans saw this in a similar vein as the indoctrination of the youth in Hitler's time.

Many believe that Obama's intention is to indoctrinate America's youth using his great power and the power and assistance of the U.S. Department of Education. A Web blogger post suggested it was for "drawing our children into the president's web of deceit enabling Obama to manipulate our youth at will." If indoctrination is Obama's intention, we will see other attempts, as he is the spider who does not quit.

The same blogger offered:

The thought that Barack Obama would have the audacity to address our children, asking our children what they, OUR CHILDREN, can do for Barack Obama comes as no surprise, but is out of place, disrespectful to the parents of OUR CHILDREN and deplorable nonetheless... Because the White House would even think of conducting themselves in this manner should give Americans pause for concern."

Chapter 5   Sin 3 of 7. The "Porkulus" Bill

Pork Guarantees Reelection - Maybe

For any Democratic Representative who had made a promise to a Mayor, or a County Commissioner, or a pack of City Councilmen, the "Porkulus Bill" was a big opportunity to come through and gain big time appreciation for the next election cycle. Some have said that the "Porkulus Bill" was just a huge candy store for the Democratic Party. People in need thought it was for them, but it was not. It was not to stimulate the economy either. It was to stimulate the opportunity for the ruling party to continue ruling -- as long as the people's complaints remained small in number.

I have heard the Porkulus Bill (aka stimulus bill) explained as something the Democrats found that was a mother-load of other people's money. They could not wait to spend it on their pet projects and to please the special interest groups who fund their campaigns. If we had no Congress, it would be much simpler to balance the budget. The Wall Street Journal did an expose on the "who benefits?" part of the bill and they found that the economy would change little after all the money was spent.

These are some of the major provisions according to the Wall Street Journal: Only 12 cents out of every dollar is for growth stimuli (which doesn't go into effect for years in some cases)

- $600 million is to buy themselves new "green" cars (even though they already spend $3 billion per year)
- $252 billion is for people who do nothing: $81 billion for Medicaid, $36 billion for unemployment benefits, $20

billion for food stamps, and $83 billion for people who don't pay income tax

- $54 billion will go to "ineffective" government programs (reported by the Office of Management and Budget or the Government Accountability Office)
- $66 billion goes to the Department of Education
- According to CNS News and Fox News there were some provisions that were far worse. Some of them did not make it into the final bill, but unfortunately, some did:
- $500 per worker and $1,000 per couple including illegal aliens since social security numbers can't be checked
- $335 million for STDs
- $4.19 billion in "neighborhood stabilization activities" such as ACORN
- $10 million for bike and walking trails
- $200 million for plug-in car stations
- $400 million for climate change research
- $600 million for grants for diesel emission reduction
- $650 million for "alternative energy technologies"
- $1.5 billion for construction of "green schools"
- $2.7 billion would go toward embryonic stem cell experimentation
- $75 million for smoking cessation
- $246 million over 11 years for investors in big budget movie projects
- $50 billion to the National Endowment for the Arts
- $150 million for bees called "honey insurance"
- $20 million for "fish barriers"

Read the Bill

I do have my own ideas on the great Obama / Mostly Democrat stimulus bill that was willingly unread and signed by my representative and your representative. I do have some ideas. However, I found the words of the master and I would like to first share these with you. On most of the "Porkulus" bill, a term offered by Rush Limbaugh to describe the excessive pork in the major stimulus bill of 2009.

Limbaugh noticed very quickly that there was more to help the reelection of our fine "honorables" than there was to help the country, which is shameful but, as noted throughout this book, very true. And, of course, those same honorables felt no shame in admitting that they indeed, did not read the bill.

Blame Bush

Nobody was denying that the country was in recession. Obama and the Democrats placed all of the blame on the Bushites and hardly mentioned the Democratic Congress that had been firing on a few missed cylinders during the last few years of the Bush Administration. Creativity cannot be based on a philosophy of "George Did It!" Rush Limbaugh acknowledged that everybody seemed to be hoping to end the reality of the recession, which according to his ditto highness, would more than likely last about five to 11 months if nobody moved.

Wrongful Intervention

Limbaugh noted that there is one trick that can change a recession from "just bad" to "really bad" and that would be the wrong kind of government intervention. Without a virtual eye blink, the Rush added that such "bad intervention" was precisely what President Barack Obama had brought forth.

The highly articulate Limbaugh expressed his thoughts as: "I don't believe this is a 'stimulus plan' at all -- I don't think it stimulates anything but the Democratic Party. This 'porkulus' bill is designed to repair the Democratic Party's power losses from the 1990s forward, and to cement the party's majority power for decades."

Even Limbaugh does not suggest that government needs to stay fully motionless. They just have to do the right thing. According to many economists and historians, and Rush Limbaugh himself, the right thing to do from the start of the "recession" was to cut tax rates. That's what you do in a recession. As a rule, it brings an economy back.

Americans Said No To Pork - Nobody Listened

Hard working Americans had a real problem with the stimulus bill as well as the bailouts. They saw their investment in the US going to things that did not matter a darn to anybody other than somebody looking for something. Our "honorable" representatives again went out of their way to show their superiority to the working class as they voted in tons of pork against the will of a vocal majority. The American people knew the pork had a high price tag and they could almost feel the price being extracted from their purses and wallets, whenever an "honorable" spoke about how honorable it was to provide for all. Regular Americans, Rush Limbaugh, regular Democrats like myself and my neighbors, all smelled the faint odor of a roasted, overdone, stinky, barbequed pig in the Washington distance. Porkulus grandidentata... etc...

Even more annoying for real Americans than the smell of burning pork, was the continuing low-ratings media blitz in support of the Obama stimulus plan. It is as if the media involved, had already determined that there was nothing wrong with pork as long as what many have called, "the chosen one" could benefit even in a small way. Eventually, the cartoonists caught up with this notion of media favoritism to the President and the Reid/ Pelosi combo, and when the cartoonist of this majestic piece wants credit, please just tell me, and you are in. See it on next page:

If you cannot see it, Figure 5-1 is a depiction of the former mainstream media outlets, referred to in this book as the low-ratings media, being attracted by the Pied Piper, the great one. The message is "follow me," but that is about it! Even if it is not true, there is clear enough reason for the folks to begin to think that it is. Nobody in the magnificent world of American media, the one-time champions of the free press, saw anything wrong with all the earmarks and all the pork and pork-ears in this bill. Why?

Maybe they were overwhelmed by the Pied Piper. It did not matter whether the enchanted were Democrat or Republican. The flutist was too good to not come forth. If you are a regular person and not an elite, then you hated the lack of veracity in the low-ratings media shown in the cartoon above. Yet, you continued. I heard you and I continue to hear you and if you have not noticed, I also make the same sounds as you do. Why are there no sounds coming from the "free" media or those sworn to keep us a free people?

Figure 5-1 The Pied Piper of the Media

Spend Spend Spend, then Spend

At Porkulus time, according to Scott Rasmussen, 59% of the people feared that Congress and the President would increase government spending way too much on frivolous line items. Not many of those that noticed then have stopped noticing now. The "Porkulus Bill" gave verification to those who feared that they were right... and then some.

The reason this goes down as a heavy mistake in the Obama mistake column, shared of course by a few Republicans and most of the Democrats in Congress who have chosen to leave their minds at home, is that despite complaint after complaint, neither the President nor Congress showed the people they mattered. They viewed the Summer Town Hall message as if it were from just few of the insignificant among us, such as you and me. Therefore, neither Congress, nor the President were compelled to sacrifice the promises they had already made to special interests. Why would they do that -- to please We the People? Since pleasing the people is low priority, they went on with business as usual, while at the same time discrediting and demeaning those who had offered legitimate dissent. Yup! That's it in a nutshell!

Chapter 6   Sin 4 of 7.   The Economy & the Auto Bailout

Oil Prices Caused the Big Recession

Most economists agree that the recession began in December, 2007. As such, this recession is much longer than most and continues to have the risk of going into a depression. More and more economists are looking back and seeing that the mortgage crisis, which precipitated the full financial crisis, may have been precipitated itself by the high cost of oil. In the summer of 2007, oil prices raged to all-time highs and consumers began to do things differently. Those that could not cut back on gasoline / oil consumption had to cut back someplace else. Everything went up in price including food, which really put a drain on a family's ability to make it through the day and night.

So, it stands to reason that the big suffering of the current recession was caused simply by high oil prices. That would mean that people defaulting on their mortgages was just another choice that had to be made -- in some cases to feed the family. So, the mortgage default issue may have only been a symptom of a far-simpler problem, high oil prices. Any of us that lived through 2007 felt the anger, saw the belt tightening, and can certainly understand the far reaching impact of the great oil price gouge of 2007/ 2008.

By May 2007, right before the summer driving season, the price of gas in the US soared to over $3.20 per gallon average US price. It went up and down though never going below $3.00 through 2007 until February 2008. From February, prices climbed like they were never going to stop, finally peaking in July 2008 at about $4.10. I am sure you remember that. From the raging oil prices of 2007, the symptoms of a major slowdown and the smell of a looming financial crisis was in the air.

Very early in 2008, some financial institutions began to fail, yet the oil and gas prices stayed high until about September, when oil prices began dropping like Obama's current approval rating (OK a lead balloon). to a low of about $1.60 per gallon in January 2009. Even without a resurging economy, the price of oil in the summer of 2009 was up to about $2.70 and when this book was written during late 2009, it was at $2.80. I predict that if oil comes down again and stay down and do not move upwards, the economy will heal itself sooner.

It was not just the US economy that got hurt by oil. Nobody got a break. The higher oil prices also caused Japan and the European states to be pulled into the recession even before the big financial problems hit. History suggests that higher oil prices started four of the last five world recessions; so why would we be surprised if the "great recession," which is still alive, was not started by oil?

Was this Really Another Great Depression?

You don't need to be an economist to answer no to that one. There seem to be enough people on Social Security, Pensions, Academics, Government Workers etc… who are keeping a portion of the other industries, including the service industries, with enough work that at least the economy is moving somewhat. Things would be much worse if this were a major depression. My cousin Tommy Rowan, a Master Plumber in Bloomfield, New Jersey and his cohort and co-worker, James Brady Jr. told me, years ago, the difference between a recession and a depression. A recession is when your neighbor is out of work and a depression is when you're out of work.

Ironically, much to the dismay of the president, VP Joe Biden said the same thing in October 2009. So, for many, this is a depression, but it is not a "great depression." Let's take a look at some of the stats that made the 1929 period a depression of the greatest magnitude that would be difficult to reproduce if somebody intended to do so.

- ✓ 1929 to 1933, production at the nation's factories, mines and utilities fell by 50%
- ✓ Auto production fell 75% from its 1929 peak
- ✓ The # of unemployed rose from 1.6 million in 1929 to 12.8 million in 1933
- ✓ 1 in 4 workers nationally were out of work at its worst
- ✓ Real disposable income fell by 28%
- ✓ Stock prices fell by 90%
- ✓ 1930 to 1933 -- Nine thousand banks failed

In late 2009, the official unemployment rate continued to rise and was just about at 10%. However, the government admitted that this number was not the real number of people out of work. There are yet another 7% who are off benefits and cannot find work and so the rate is thus 17%, and perhaps this statistic is soberingly close to 25% or 1 in 4 as in the valley of the Great Depression.

Production is down about 15% but there has been a slowing and even a bit of a turnaround in the last months of 2009. Autos are down substantially but the clunker program did help sales in the third quarter. Production is not as bad as it was in the Great Depression and Ford, the American car hero company, is doing better than all others.

Disposable income for those who get jobs in other industries is down significantly, but those who have held on to their jobs have not seen a marked decline. Finally, just about 300 battered banks and thrifts have either failed or are on their way so despite its issues, the TARP has had some effect on this statistic. Of course with only about 8500 banks in the US, if we had 9000 failures it would be a miracle.

Can Obama Handle a Poor Economy

The fact is, it is much easier to operate when the economy is good than when it is bad. It is much easier to be President when the economy is good than when it is bad. When things are bad, it is tough to operate at the highest level of efficiency or focus tightly on the most profitable or the most beneficial activities. Companies and governments that watch the economy turn downward and yet continue to operate as they did in more bountiful times can quickly run into trouble. Refocusing and rebalancing can help companies and thus governments ride out the stresses of a downturn be prepared for improvements when the time is right.

For businesses, today's challenges are great. The financial markets are unstable; commodity prices are in flux; housing, automotive and other industries are still fighting for survival, despite billions of aid. For the government, the deficit is crippling and the risk of a major inflation looms on the horizon. And, so any cavalier approach to managing the country's finances, such as bailing out the auto industry to save union pensions or providing taxpayer money for car purchases or to take taxpayer owned "clunkers" after the trade-in and destroy them rather than make them available to the "less fortunate," are viewed with a wary eye by the general public. When you can't afford it, you simply don't do it. But, we have!

The actions of a President and his economic advisors do have a major effect on the economy and it is not always as intended. They have more of an effect when the dollars are measured in trillions. Look at the following facts: In the period right after the Obama election in November 2008 through mid-February 2009, the Dow Jones fell 18%. You may recall that this was during a period in which the Congress and the Obama Administration-to-be were discussing their stimulus plans and then ultimately implementing them. Ironically, the 18% drop was larger than the September through October plunge during the Bush administration.

George Did It! But Did He Really?

In January 2009, when the Obama plan, which was reasonably well understood by then, promised far greater deficits than the two much smaller 'emergency stimulus' plans signed by President George W. Bush in 2008, the market literally tanked. It was the worst January performance in 113 years. Of course the Obama machine attributed all of the bad market performance to "George did it!"

The market is just one indicator, but it is has not been very favorable to Obamanomics, and it will more than likely get worse before it gets better. The new President immediately went about turning what were bad economic times into extremely long and horrible economic times. The Obama remedy is just about exactly what one would do if they wanted to bring the economy of the US down and they had the power to do so. Critics examined with a wary eye the motivations of this President in enacting and supporting plans that have never worked in the past. Can the President's sheer magnanimity make bad plans work well?

The spending is nothing less than massive, irrational, and wasteful and it is turning the economy southward, not towards recovery. With the largest government spending bill in American history under his belt, Obama and the Congress embraced this bill, which was riddled with pork, and they rushed to sign it, though most had no clue what was written between page 1 and page 1132 of this historically poor legislation.

At the time, Obama admitted the bill was not perfect and set the White House chief apologist in motion with the spin. Robert Gibbs said Obama wouldn't be the first President to sign legislation that he viewed as less than ideal. And so that chapter of American History was closed while the budget was busting at the seams.

Jefferson and Obama

I am a big fan of Thomas Jefferson. In subsequent chapters, I offer a number of other quotes from the Founding Fathers. Before we continue our look at the current economic scenario, called Obamanomics (also called income redistribution by some cynics - hah!), of the sitting President and his team, it's time to indulge in a few more of those flashes back in history, as reminders of from whence we came.

Thomas Jefferson always believed that a man's toil should be his own, unless he gives it up for his own reasons. "To take from one, because it is thought his own industry and that of his father has acquired too much, in order to spare to others who have not exercised equal industry and skill, is to violate arbitrarily the first principle of association, 'to guarantee to everyone a free exercise of his industry and the fruits acquired by it.' "

The Constitution is contained in its entirety in Appendix A. The preamble of the Constitution establishes the goal of the whole democracy effort as to; "establish justice, insure domestic tranquility, provide for the common defense, promote the general welfare, and secure the blessings of liberty to ourselves and our posterity." Note that there is no mention of taking from the possessions of one to give to another.

It does not take a genius to find that there are a number of US citizens today who believe, with good reason, that our President and his CZARS are either avowed communists, socialists, Marxists, or some other "ist" or their philosophies and leanings at least would cause one to conclude they are practicing "ists." The "ist" notion means the individuals no longer have relevance and instead everything is for the good of the state. This would have brought Jefferson either to an early death or he would have hopped on the next ship back to England.

Think about the published backgrounds of the President's CZARS, if you will and even what you are hearing when the

President speaks. Obama is on TV almost every hour of every day, or so it seems, so if you missed this point, please let me know! Just turn your TV on and see if the Prez is not there talking about helping somebody else with your money. That's Obamanomics and he has already begun to take your money with the heavy give-aways and bail-outs, and the pork. Nowhere in the Constitution does it give him, or anybody else, the right to do that.

Charity Is Not for Government

So that you do not start thinking that I think the President is a revolutionary, which of course would make me a confirmed nutcase, though he has yet to prove otherwise, the basic tenet of Marxism is the same feel-good stuff that those on the left continually preach. Yet, the charitable donation line on the lefty's own personal tax returns, including VP Joe Biden, shows that they do not believe that the funding of their favorite projects should come from their own wallets. They are not compelled to contribute to their own goals and they give little to charity.

In the preamble, the founders mention the notion of the "general welfare." This is not to mean welfare as far as help for the needy! This is the phrase that the income redistribution crowd use to validate their rationalized right to your stuff. To stretch this to the level of income redistribution sought by the feel-good crowd, it would have to imply that the Founding Fathers had a Marxist view of the Federal Government. It would mean that the Feds have the duty and the power to "take from each according to his ability, and give to each according to his need."

Big Government Doesn't Work.

In a democracy, is it the duty of the government to define and measure out individual well-being against the will of some on behalf of others? This is not only very dangerous to the basic concepts of liberty and freedom; it is diametrically at odds with everything the Founders believed and wrote.

To this end, Jefferson also wrote, "I predict future happiness for Americans if they can prevent the government from wasting the labors of the people under the pretense of taking care of them." Jefferson "knew" that Obama was coming, "A democracy is nothing more than mob rule, where fifty-one percent of the people may take away the rights of the other forty-nine." This time, because the Bush years were blasted daily by the popular low-ratings media, and because the economy was in the toilet by the time the election was over, Obama got a little less than 53% and Bush got just about 46%. That sets the stage for an Obama style "Mob Rule."

If you have read any of my other works, you would know that I have no great love for huge corporations. They bleed society for all they can get and give back little. And for as much as I hate big corporations, there is still one thing worse than big corporations, big government. Big government can create laws to take all you have to give to those they deem needy. Big Government does not work. David Woods knows this and has written about how ludicrous the very idea of big government is. Check out his eye opening piece when you have time:

http://www.lewrockwell.com/orig7/woods-d2.html.

Here is a sample:

> *"There is this unwritten assumption that, given any problem or bad news of any kind, that government politicians and bureaucrats know what's best for all of us; that anyone who works for the government is, by definition, smarter, wiser, and has more honesty and integrity. And so, every time something bad happens, they all respond with that all-too-predictable knee-jerk response that, by golly, the government needs to DO SOMETHING about it! And inevitably, the government*

DOES indeed do something: it gets bigger and more powerful, and spends more money." ...

Barack Obama and his team of "ists" think Woods is wrong. But, then again they have to or they would have no purpose. Obama is a modern day Robin Hood who wants to take from the rich and give to his rich friends and rich Obama-friendly corporations, and oh, yes, and the poor if there are any left. No matter how much you make, big or small, you run the risk that with one stroke of a pen, you will become rich in name only. Your income will not have increased but your share of the government tab will go up. You can bet all the ink in the world on that. J. B. Williams writing about Obamanomics 101 notes the following:

"when those who pay little or no taxes at all (most Americans) get to define "fair share" in the tax code, they will seek out a small target (the rich – top 2%) with deep pockets."

Soon, you too will be rich as the percentage increases. Williams also writes,

"Property rights are at the foundation of individual liberty and personal freedom and our government was formed for the primary purpose of protecting and preserving individual freedom via protecting the right of every individual to earn and own property. Yet it is the principles of Marxism that drive Obamanomics and rule economic policy via democratic mob mentality today... class warfare and punitive measures against our nation's most productive and most defenseless citizens... It is not enough to protect only yourself from continued affronts on individual freedom and liberty. You must be willing to protect and defend the freedoms and liberties of others in order to protect and preserve your own."

Neal Boortz does not want to be quoted from this particular speech regarding his views on Obamanomics. He once wrote a college commencement address which is very powerful but he, unfortunately, has never been invited to give the address at a real institution. Here are a few lines that make some of the points in this section:

> *"So here are the first assignments for your initial class in reality: Pay attention to the news, read newspapers, and listen to the words and phrases that proud Liberals use to promote their causes. Then compare the words of the left to the words and phrases you hear from those evil, heartless, greedy conservatives. From the Left you will hear 'I feel.' From the Right you will hear 'I think.' From the Liberals you will hear references to groups --The Blacks, The Poor, The Rich, The Disadvantaged, The Less Fortunate. From the Right you will hear references to individuals. On the Left you hear talk of group rights; on the Right, individual rights.*
>
> *That about sums it up, really: Liberals feel. Liberals care. They are pack animals whose identity is tied up in group dynamics. Conservatives and Libertarians think -- and, setting aside the theocracy crowd, their identity is centered on the individual.*
>
> *Liberals feel that their favored groups have enforceable rights to the property and services of productive individuals. Conservatives (and Libertarians, myself among them I might add) think that individuals have the right to protect their lives and their property from the plunder of the masses.*
>
> *In college you developed a group mentality, but if you look closely at your diplomas you will see that they have your individual names on them. Not the name of your school mascot,*

or of your fraternity or sorority, but your name. Your group identity is going away. Your recognition and appreciation of your individual identity starts now....

Enjoy the rest at:
http://boortz.com/more/commencement.html

Obama's big economic mistake then was being the real Obama. If he had masked his "ist" views for a bit longer he might have been able to sneak in his whole agenda before the masses woke up. Obamanomics is the economics permitted by ists. That's about it.

Yes, This Chapter Is also About the Auto Bailout

Besides the big debacles with the bank bailouts and the "Porkulus" bill, as well as the overall insidiousness of the whole Obamanomics thing as described above, the auto companies have taken their toll on the US taxpayer. You may remember a time, of course, when GM was a successful company. May I ask if you know about them ever offering a deal in which a thousand sick kids from across the country would get to go to Disney? Do you know of GM donating to church groups performing charitable work? Do you know of GM ever trying to find the most worthy person in the US, and maybe a number of people like that person and maybe, just maybe, give them one of the company's products -- such as a nice car, for their work for mankind?

Me neither! Yet, when GM, the one-time largest corporation in America was in trouble, they looked to the Treasury of the people to bail them out of their jam. Most of the people said, "no" but none of that mattered to our Congress or to Barack Hussein Obama, who owed the auto unions a favor and found your dollars as a fine way to pay them back.

The Obama Administration created debt that is so large that taxpayers, in many ways, are immune to feeling emotion about its excessiveness, along with the raging budget deficits. No, it is not because the Chinese are so nice! It is because we are, one and all, sick of Congress and the Obama Administration giving away all of what Americans have worked for -- for so many years and frittering it away. Not only is he messing with us, but how about taking away from those Americans who have not even been born. Won't they be surprised at what a nice world their parents left to them?

Government Motors - Friend of the ~~People~~ State

US Taxpayers face huge losses on most of the $81 billion in taxpayer aid that was given to the auto industry, despite objections from the owners of the National Treasury, the American taxpayers. Oversight panels have suggested that the chances that John Q. Public will ever be paid back for the largesse of Congress and Obama towards the auto industry and the auto unions really don't look good.

In one of the Congressional Oversight Panel reports in 2009, for example, the regulators offered that they felt that most of the $23 billion initially provided to General Motors Corp. and Chrysler LLC during late 2008 was unlikely ever to be repaid. Despite the probability of a big loss for the taxpayers, the panel congratulated Barack Obama for having driven a hard bargain, even though it would probably not be enough.

They chose not to mention that American taxpayers, who, of course, are the ultimate bill payers, were never interested in GM getting a bailout dime in the first place. $Twenty-three billion was gone and, nobody got fired. Well, of course the President did fire the CEO of GM, but, remember, the government does not want to be in the car business.

Despite its purported desire to let things alone, the Obama government now is the proud owner of 10 percent of Chrysler and 61 percent of GM. Many agree that this is a direct result of Obama's quest for more power than had ever been amassed by any president, ever! Though the two companies are still listed privately, for taxpayer shareholders to ever be paid back, the shares must be made public and they must appreciate very sharply in order that "We the People," the unwilling investors, have our money put back in our treasury.

So far Ford, which got nothing, is doing well, and the duopoly of Bailout Motors -- GM and Chrysler, are still sustaining big losses.

Is There Really Oversight?

Who is the government oversight panel? The Congressional Oversight Panel was created as part of TARP. It was designed to provide an additional layer of oversight, beyond the Special Inspector General for the TARP and regular audits by the Government Accountability Office.

The panel's report recommends that the Treasury Department consider placing its (our) auto company holdings into an independent trust, to avoid any "conflicts of interest." Of course, you and I know there would be no conflict of interest if the government (our representatives) had exercised the will of the people, instead of the will of special interests. Who trusts government today?

Every now and then, you find an honest person speaking out about what they know is wrong. Among the members of the Congressional Oversight Panel is a person named Jeb Hensarling, a Texas Republican Congressman. Hensarling dissented from the report. Maybe he did not like Obama getting praise for the $23 Billion loss. I don't think he dissented so that the Prez could get an AIG-sized bonus for his extracurricular management duties in the auto industry.

Anyway, Hensarling had a big problem with the auto companies receiving any taxpayer funding and he criticized the government for picking market "winners and losers." Thank you Jeb! The big losers, of course, are the taxpayers, as the Congressional Budget Office estimated in June 2009 that taxpayers were about to lose about $40 billion of the first $55 billion in aid. Sounds like a lot of reason for praising our elected officials?

A CEO with Government Pull

With a $50 Billion giveaway to GM, and the forming of what to some is now Government Motors, the new, de facto CEO, Barack Hussein Obama, in fact, pulled a power play early in the game. Many Americans remember that Obama decided that the GM CEO had to go. How else could he be the CEO if there already was a CEO? After a bit of government strong-arming, Rick Wagoner, the former CEO, fired by Obama, left peaceably in mid July 2009 after having been retained for four months while the company figured out his exit package.

Wagoner got almost $8.2 million under a pension settlement plus a nice $74,030 annual pension. Many in the American taxpayer community would love to receive a few million without even having the historical legacy of destroying what was once the largest corporation in the world.

Should Wagoner have gotten fired? Yes, he should have been fired, but long before President Obama got the honors. In corporations, the board of directors fires and hires CEOs, not the President of the United States. In America, many of us know that the President of the US does not have the Constitutional authority to fire anybody from a private company, while it is still a private company.

Obama exercised unbridled power in this instance and that has many, who have concerns for what else the President thinks he can do without explicit authority, quite worried.. Always the great orator and excuse maker, the President did "assure" America that General Motors executives and board members would be the ones making business decisions, not the government.

One has to wonder as to how much autonomy the GM officers actually have, seeing as the "non-decision making government" went as far as to fire the last GM CEO. Think about it.

Though GM the company was not loved or unloved by most Americans, their brands like Buick, Chevy and Cadillac had all been American symbols. They are expected to continue being American symbols, but with less love from Americans, since GM is now a failed company, and perhaps even worse, a government controlled company. To get some more cash from a non-government source, GM had been trying, for many months, to sell its Hummer division. Most know the Hummer as a luxury makeover of the US military HMMWV or Hum-Vee as it is called.

They found a buyer, Sichuan Tengzhong Heavy Industrial Machinery Company Ltd from mainland China. Does this mean the Chinese will be making American War vehicles?

Right now, before the sale is concluded to China, the military and commercial versions run on the same GM assembly line. The luxury Hummer gets special treatment after that and the military Hummer often goes for special armor. Surely, the Chinese will appreciate their dual role of owner of the U.S.A. and manufacturer of US war machines.

GM - Legacy to Nothing

From better than 51 percent of the car and truck industry in the world to a failed entity; that is the summation of the GM legacy. The little green cars that many think will become the final GM swansong are a part of the government's social engineering for the good of the world environment. Whether it will be good for GM as a capitalist firm, of course, is questionable. In the meantime, hang on to your wallets. They'll probably need a lot more.

The government knew that taxpayers wanted no stake in a GM bailout. In November, 2008, just after the election, 45% of Americans were opposed to the loans, 35% favored them, and 20% were undecided. Almost all Americans (80%) were concerned the government would get too involved in the private economy. Now, with the energy grab with Cap and Trade, and the healthcare grab and the Porky Pig bill, it appears that the new Obama government wants lots and lots of power and this has lots and lots of Americans very concerned, and rightfully so.

Back in late 2008, 48% of Americans did not buy the idea that GM was too big to fail. As a rule, Americans believed that it was better for the economy to let companies like General Motors that had become inept with no help from the people, fail rather than providing subsidies from the people to keep them in business.

At first, when a brave Congress rejected the first big auto bailout package, for the first time in a long time, our Congress received a higher approval rating from Americans. Admittedly, it was still at a dismal level. Americans do get it. Congress, unfortunately, as we have discussed many times in this book, does not get it at all.

In 2009, 67% of voters were opposed to the plan that provided GM with billions in federal funding and gave the government its majority ownership interest. Congress must know something we do not know. Why would Congress and the fresh President go ahead with the bailouts in spite of public opposition?

Congress Is for Congress

There are other polls that Congress considers before making decisions, specifically those reflecting the opinions of the owner class, the corporations and also special interests. For Congress and the President and the parties listed in the prior sentence to be almost in lockstep on bailing out the auto companies, something stunk rotten in Peoria. The interest of We the people were the last considered because there are lots of others on the list before us.

Our "honorable" representatives and the President choose the other team on a consistent basis anymore. This is what happened with the auto bailout. It's like We the People just aren't even there. Maybe it's time to bail out the stink from the halls of Congress? A 545 person cleaning perhaps is just what the doctor ordered. How about 2010? And don't think your own greedy congressman doesn't have to go.

Ford-- an American Company-- Proud of It!

Ford is now the folk hero of many Americans, and for good reason. For as much as their counterparts, GM and Chrysler, cried and ignored the very ideals of the same capitalism that had once helped to make them Auto Superpowers, Ford worked harder and made tough choices and stood by the good old' fashioned American work ethic to get themselves out of their own financial dilemma. Once a Chevy man, I currently own my big, roomy, (energy efficient?) Expedition that I use to tote my large extended family to places hither and yon, as well as my smaller sized Lincoln Town Car, which are magnificent machines. I can honestly say I am tickled to drive any of my Fords lately. Bravo Ford! Thank you for not seeking federal help.

Taxpayers have Ford and do not need GM. Moreover, the statistics suggest that 61% of Americans think Ford is more likely to survive than Chrysler or GM. Additionally, 76% of voters now are convinced that it is more than possible for the US economy to recover even if GM goes out of business. Americans have grown feistier each time Congress turns its back on what's good for the public.

We are sick of the "what's good for Congress" idea. Americans who are Americans have clearly decided that what's good for General Motors or Government Motors is not good for the country after all.

With all these new David's emerging in public, exercising their American rights, has anybody seen Goliath recently? Let's hope he keeps hiding. We don't need him, no how!

Chapter 7 Sin 5 of 7. CZARS, Cronies & Snitches

Who Ya Gonna Call, CZAR-busters! Can't Get No Help Nowhere!

Much has been made of President Obama's controversial appointments (as many as 44 by some estimates) to the very inexact position of CZARs. While the mere fact of their existence cannot be used to demonstrate some sort of conspiratorial intent, reasoned citizens must surely question the motivation behind some of these questionable selections.

Perhaps more importantly, nearly a year into the Obama Presidency, roughly 40% of key cabinet positions remained unfilled, many of these in the areas of defense and security. Former Pentagon Comptroller, Dov Zakheim, offered his thoughts on the lack of defense appointments,

> *"This is very worrisome, the Secretary [Robert Gates] has a problem."*

Another Previous Defense Department miffintiff, Jacques Gansler states:

> *[Filling the jobs] certainly has gone slower than I expected, especially considering the acquisition and service vacancies at a time when the country is fighting two wars and with the budget issues the Pentagon is facing.*

CZARS and CZARinas

In normal administrations, the President selects people to oversee or coordinate key positions. These positions may be of particular interest to the administration, and normally nobody even notices. It is worrisome that all of these CZARS are showing up out of the blue, mostly unconfirmed by Congress, occupying powerful positions in the Administration. How is it that we have these instead of those? Those of course are what we would expect, like, the Cabinet for example. Why are these CZARS there first appearing to be in lieu of vital, Senate-confirmed posts that have always been the integral components of our government?

While most of the low-ratings media ignores this big issue, Fox News, especially the former CNN star, Glenn Beck, have initiated what might be called an all-out assault on the President's new czars. With somewhat less fervor, some in Congress have noticed and are starting to ask questions.

One particular representative, Patrick McHenry (great name) called for a hearing on the roles and responsibilities of the Obamaczars. Like many, McHenry was concerned that the czars have high-level, decision-making authority as their non-czar titles indicated. He and many others wonder how this is happening without a regimen of Senate Hearings in which their backgrounds can be examined and their suitability for their positions can be determined. Was the president circumventing Congress' Constitutionally-mandated confirmation process? McHenry attacked the notion on a second front and asserted that if the czars were given no actual power, he was equally concerned that we, the taxpayers were fronting the bill for the salaries of these apparent symbols of authority. I might feel more comfortable, but irritated all the same if the latter were true.

Jack Kingston, R-Ga said:

It's almost like the president is building a parallel government, one that's in the constitution and then one that is outside of the constitution and the authority of congress.

Administrative Actions Are Not Always Understandable

Sometimes, unexpectedly, Harry Reid or somebody in the administration gets an untreatable bug and the next thing you know something unexpected is happening. In mid-September 2009, out of nowhere, one of the Obamaczars, Cass Sunstein somehow was up before the Senate for confirmation. The way Reid and the Senate treated this was at the same level of importance as one of the Paige's ordering a latte or a coffee. The Cass Sunstein confirmation told me that the Senate cannot be trusted in confirming czars. Where were the questions, gentlemen and ladies?

One of the puzzles that I have had regarding the Cass Sunstein senatorial confirmation is, why it was done. If most czars are not confirmed by the Senate and it is lawful that they not be, what made the Sunstein confirmation necessary? You can ask yourself if you think that everybody involved was looking for political cover or is this required by law? The crispiest source I could find on the subject comes from Wharton County Junior College (WCJC). They are a two year, comprehensive community college offering a wide range of postsecondary educational programs and services including Associate programs. As part of syllabus material for a Government Course on the Federal Bureaucracy, they offer readable faculty/ student notes at the following URL:.

http://facultyweb.wcjc.edu/users/eMcLane/Government%202 302/Syllabus/The%20Federal%20Bureaucracy.doc

Unless you have a predisposition for pain, you will not want to absorb all of the stuff they provide. Political Science courses and government courses are great courses for all college students to take. The only issue I would have, being a sitting Assistant Professor at a small university, is that these courses are full of liberal thought indoctrination as much as information about the political process.

Most of us already know about the separation of powers and the Constitution and the simple things of government. In today's Obama world, we actually have to know more. We have to have a clue about this huge bureaucracy known as the federal government. Their mission is to take the pages of the bills that are passed, and after getting an interpretation, creating the proper subsection into the proper bureaucratic entity to assure the law is carried out.

Obama is stretching the meaning of bureaucracy, but on any given day in Wharton County, the outline of the Washington Bureaucracy, as it existed on that day, was there for all to see. For those that don't like fact chucked lists, move on past this section. For those that do, this is our bureaucracy, bloated though it may be.

The Federal Bureaucracy

Organization of the Bureaucracy

- The federal bureaucracy is part of the executive branch.
- The Constitution is silent about the organization of the bureaucracy.
- Congress and the president have created the executive departments, commissions, agencies, and bureaus of the federal bureaucracy on a piecemeal basis over the last 200 years through the legislative process.

Cabinet Departments

- Require Senate Confirmation
- Independent Executive Agencies

- Such as NASA, CIA, EPA
- Subject to Senate confirmation, president appoints their heads.

Government Corporations (Quasi)

- Postal Service
- AMTRAK
- FDIC
- directed by boards appointed by the president, pending Senate confirmation.

Foundations and Institutes

- National Science Foundation
- National Endowment for the Arts.
- Appointed by the president -- no confirmation

Independent Regulatory Commissions

- FTC
- FCC
- SEC
- Appointed by the president with Senate appr

Quasi-Governmental Companies

- Federal National Mortgage Association (Fannie Mae)
- Federal Home Loan Mortgage Corporation (Freddie Mac)
- etc...
- Organized as corporation
- Board of Directors appoints CEO
- Board members elected as in other corporations

Rulemaking

- Independent regulatory commissions and other regulatory agencies
- No senate approval necessary

Politics and Administration

The President

- Presidents have an important stake in the faithful and efficient implementation of federal programs, but they must work to influence the administrative process, and their success is not assured.

- Presidents have several tools for influencing the bureaucracy.

   1. The president has the authority to name most of the top administrators in the bureaucracy.

   2. The president can use the Office of Management and Budget (OMB) to evaluate agency performance and screen rules proposed by executive branch agencies.

3. The president proposes agency budgets to
Congress...

Politics and Administration

Congress

- Congress has strong legal authority to oversee the actions of the
  federal bureaucracy. After all, Congress created the various
  bureaucratic agencies and delegated authority to them.
- What Congress gives, Congress can take away...

Interest Groups

- Every agency has several or perhaps dozens of interest groups vitally
  concerned about the programs it administers...

Bureaucrats

- Bureaucrats have interests of their own, separate from those of the
  president, members of Congress, and interest groups.
- Bureaucrats have resources for defending their turf...

Conclusion: The Federal Bureaucracy and Public Policy

The federal bureaucracy participates in every stage of the policymaking
process. Agencies sometimes focus attention on issues through public reports
and statements.

They help the White House and Congress formulate and adopt policy
through their lobbying efforts in both branches. Finally, while the
bureaucracy's central mission is the implementation of public policy, it also
evaluates policies once they are in place.

Founding Fathers v. CZARS -- Why?

President Obama has named lots and lots of czars. Nobody would say that, if properly utilized, czars can be an effective way to address issues. Other presidents have appointed them, for sure. The problem is that because zuwiel ist zuwiel, overuse can be reckless and can create lots of problems, both real and perceptive.

Big Issues With CZARS

Appointed Czars typically do not get screened by the US Senate. A vigilant Senate (sorry) can assure Americans that poor candidates are weeded out. Cabinet members and many other sub cabinet jobs do need senate confirmation. Hopefully senators do a better job of checking them out than they did with Cass Sunstein.

In most cases, without Senate confirmation, there is not even a whimper of a check or balance for the people to assure personal agendas are not in control. And, if that is not enough, other than in Czarist Russia before the Bolshevik Revolution, too many czars are more than likely unconstitutional as the President gets to bypass the Senate and the Constitution

Many have no idea even today who Van Jones is. He was a racist and a man who called Republicans, "assholes" in public. He offered a number of theories as to how "whitey" was running the world. He resigned during Saturday Night Live, or so it seems.

Looking at the Van Jones "resignation" gives any of us adequate reason for being concerned about all czars. Does the fact that he resigned on a Saturday night in the middle of a 3 day holiday weekend show that the transparent Administration had something they wanted most people to miss.

They did not want anybody to know. Could David Axelrod, the most powerful man in the world as he runs the Obama machine, have been trying to bury the story? Look hard at the Cass Sunstein appointment and confirmation by the Senate and you must ask if Senators really can do anything right. He glided through with minimal discussion.

Do You Trust Your Government?

A big concern that I hear over and over again is that people do not trust the government and the czars make them uneasy. After the Romanovs, who were real czars, the then new Soviet Russia and Nazi Germany both called these types of "managers," commissars. Of course the president calls them czars. No matter what they are called, at best they are vague, undefined shadows appointed by the "Leader" to carry out his intentions. This happens to be the same definition as that for "commissar." This term understandably is not used in this government, nor is the more friendly term, comrade.

From the history of America, we know that the US is a constitutional republic. In such a form of rule, the government (rulers) does not have a role in every part of everyday administration of employee life.

Instead the Congress creates various departments, agencies and administrations. The bureaucracy discussion above demonstrates this. Everything that the federal government does must, in some way, relate to its powers under the Constitution.

Over the years, the role of the President's Cabinet has increased. The first cabinet offices were very clear in purpose -- diplomacy, war, justice, money, and even postal services. Only administrative areas that Congress assures are constitutional are created and work can then be done under the role of government. Congress is the branch that does this work.

I might suggest that this is the very heartbeat of limited government. Presidential appointments to major leadership areas not approved by Congress could very easily be considered unconstitutional if our representatives were really doing their jobs.

There are no "Thought Police," for example, authorized by congress, nor are there snitch departments in which neighbors can report on the activities of neighbors. We know that Germany had its SS and the Reichstag and there was the Central Committee of the Communist party to do things like this but we don't really have things like that in America because of our Constitution. The reason we do not have such bureaus like the Politburo, for example, is because Congress is independent of the President and vice versa. We also have the Supreme Court serving as perhaps an unequal partner.

This structure (separation of powers) is a natural check (and balancing agent) upon the notion of a statist government with an executive, such as a president at the top. Our President has Congress and the Supreme Court to limit his or her powers. Unchecked executive power is the form of government that we would find in the "ists" described in earlier sections of this chapter.

Our representative constitutional democracy, thankfully, does not permit this but since unconstitutional things are happening before our eyes today, somebody brave must rise up complain to end those things that are unconstitutional. If it is a democrat, today at least, they will be heard. And, all of our government leaders must pay heed.

Congress is very complicit in the permitting of the Obamaczars to function even though it compromises the Congress's own authority. Congress, in the stroke of a pen, with its oversight powers can create and/or destroy executive branch departments or quasi-departments such as the czardoms. As a point of note, the Congress, especially the House, which collectively is the direct representative branch of the people in the government, can also create and destroy federal courts or change their jurisdictions. It can also increase or decrease the size of the Supreme Court. Watch out for that one.

Additionally, Congress has the money and can set budgets and spend money. Congress sets the budgets and gives out the funds for other parts of the federal government. When Congress does not act in the people's best interests, it is our duty to let them know and then find suitable candidates to replace them in the next election. That time has come.

With so much power, can the Congress find fault with an appointed czar or commissar who holds a position not created by Congress? The answer is that the Congress has no control as they formally do not hold an office or a congressionally approved position. The individual can resign, as Van Jones did (some think with perhaps a modicum of coaxing) or the President can fire them. But, what if the president chooses not to fire a czar at Congress's request? This can cause a constitutional crisis and thus, among many other reasons, the czars are dangerous for the country.

As an aside, there would be a constitutional crisis if all branches of government chose to ignore the constitution to further their collusive ends. Because three branches must be in collusion, it is difficult to imagine constitutional violations over the long haul. However, if the active branches, legislative and executive, choose to ignore or worse yet, foster unconstitutional activities, there would more than likely be a long period before the courts could solve the problem. In that interim, the country itself would be at risk.

The leader of the US, in this case Barack Obama, can become more than the office itself. Over time, with this unauthorized and un-monitored structure, the government can begins to parallel the structure of the party in control. Do you think Barack Obama has too much power or is it just that he is on TV every day?

Ask yourself if you know of any legislators from the past who have actually "voted" for legislation not yet written. This is rather Stalinesque, don't you think? Even Judicial nominees offer little more than a pretense of adhering to ideals of impartial administration of justice and the Constitution.

Are commissars (czars) replacing the functions of Cabinet Secretaries without Congress's OK? Probably not, I hope, but it does not look right and it does not smell right! All of this is troubling. One means of reigning in all this power is to stop permitting the President to define all the changes. Congress must exercise its due roll of protecting the people it serves from an aggressive executive branch.

If we look at the health bill as an example, Congress has not done too well with the health bill. They don't even take the time to read the bills anymore. The cause for concern, of course is that without Congressional Oversight and discussion about vital issues, our President, Barack Hussein Obama, is not just appointing dozens and dozens of "czars." He is creating a party-state system of political commissars. Can you imagine the plans these folks can have for us?

Consider that with or without czars, an executive leader of a government may behave in ways that are not within their power. We see that today in the current implementation of the US executive branch. Think of these types of leaders as you examine our current situation.

- Despot
- Oppressive Leader
- Tyrant
- Dictator

Despot: An innocuous description of a despot is "a ruler with absolute power." Though dangerous, this is not as bad as the second definition which is "a person who wields power oppressively, such as a tyrant.

Oppressive Leader: Difficult to bear; burdensome; Exercising power arbitrarily and often unjustly; tyrannical.

Tyrant:. An absolute ruler who governs without restrictions; A ruler who exercises power in a harsh, cruel manner. An oppressive, harsh, arbitrary person.;

Dictator: A person exercising absolute power -- a ruler who has absolute, unrestricted control in a government without hereditary succession.

From all of this information, you can probably craft a definition for czar that would scare the living daylights out of both you and me. Think of these words being in the combined definition: person, absolute power, rules oppressively, harsh, cruel, arbitrary, actions are burdensome, and weigh heavily on the spirit.

Do you think as the czars find out how much power they really have been given by the president that they will treat We the People like a pastor tending his or her flock, or like a lion tamer, assuring that there is enough fire in the lions by restricting their ability to exercise freedom?

Obama and the 40 + CZARS

These are the czars that are on the list as of the end of 2009 / beginning of 2010. It would not help my case to show the changes in the guard so I leave the list as it was when the first version was printed. It is just as telling as today's list.

- ✓ President of Czars & the People – Barack Hussein Obama
- ✓ AIDS Czar – Jeffrey Crowley
- ✓ Afghanistan Czar: Richard Holbrooke

- ✓ Auto Recovery Czar: Ed Montgomery
- ✓ Border Czar – Alan Bersin
- ✓ California Water Czar: David J. Hayes
- ✓ Car Czar – Steven Rattner then Ron Bloom
- ✓ Central Region Czar: Dennis Ross
- ✓ Climate/Energy Czar – Carol Browner - also Environment Czar
- ✓ Compensation Czar – Kenneth Feinberg
- ✓ Copyright Czar – Not appointed yet
- ✓ Domestic Violence Czar: Lynn Rosenthal
- ✓ Drug Czar – Gil Kerlikowske
- ✓ Economic Czar – Paul Volcker
- ✓ Education Czar – Arne Duncan
- ✓ Energy and Environment Czar: Carol Browner -- also Climate/Energy Czar
- ✓ Faith-based Czar – Joshua DuBois
- ✓ Guantanamo Closure Czar - Daniel Fried
- ✓ Great Lakes Czar – Cameron Davis
- ✓ Green Jobs Czar - Van Jones - resigned
- ✓ Health-care Czar – Nancy-Ann DeParle
- ✓ Housing Czar – Noli 'Kabayan' de Castro
- ✓ Infotech Czar - Vivek Kundra
- ✓ Intelligence Czar – Adm Dennis Blair
- ✓ Manufacturing Czar Ron Bloom, also the Car Czar
- ✓ Mortgage Czar – Not appointed yet - clearly not a priority
- ✓ Pay Czar – Kenneth Feinberg
- ✓ Rationing Czar -- Ezekiel Emanuel
- ✓ Regulatory Czar – Cass Sunstein
- ✓ Safe Schools Czar Robert Jennings
- ✓ Science Czar: John Holdren
- ✓ Stimulus Accountability Czar – Earl Devaney
- ✓ Sudan Czar: J. Scott Gration
- ✓ TARP Czar – Herb Allison
- ✓ Technology Czar – Aneesh Chopra
- ✓ Terrorism Czar – John Brennan
- ✓ Urban Czar – Adolfo Carrion
- ✓ Weapons Czar: Ashton Carter
- ✓ WMD Czar – Gary Samore

In the first version of this book, I felt it was necessary to explain the czars. None of which I am aware became independent of the president and none began to speak to the press on his behalf. So I am not including detailed info on any of them in this book. There should be no czars...period!

White House Snitches

The fact is that less and less Americans trust their government and with good reason. Every day there is a new reason to feel wary of the reach of Uncle Sam. A recent attack on free speech occurred the summer of 2009. One could easily get the idea that the White House had just repealed on its own, the First Amendment. The Obama Administration had asked neighbors to forward emails they received about the Administration from friends and colleagues and neighbors directly to the White House. For what purpose? To send out the black car and take the offenders to the gulags?

Senator John Cornyn (R-TX) wrote to President Obama expressing his concerns about this matter. The issue arises from a White House blog written by Macon Phillips, who is an official guy in the Administration. He is the White House Director of New Media, a sorta-miniczar. Phillips noted that there had been a lot of disinformation about health insurance reform out there both on the Web and floating around in chain emails.

Showing deep concern for this, he stated that since the White House could not keep track of all of them, "we're asking for your help. If you get an email or see something on the web about health insurance reform that seems fishy, send it to flag@whitehouse.gov." Astonishing!

What a great new spy scheme. And, without the help of Bill Cosby and Robert Culp, the original stars of the hit TV show from the 1960's "I Spy," Phillips thought he could slip this little guy under the radar. He was wrong. In a nutshell, the White House was asking you to report on your neighbors, family, and friends who might disagree with the President's policy choices on healthcare.

It was Barack Hussein Obama at the helm. Additionally, with just a little more reading you could also find that The White House was also implying that you should think twice before sending an email disagreeing with the President, since the cohorts of Barack Hussein Obama might end up getting your email, and then what will you do, Hah?

The White House email address says it all. "*flag*@whitehouse.gov. Hey, let's flag those who disagree with us... great idea... just a little unconstitutional. For what purpose are these individuals being flagged? In his letter, Senator Cornyn rightly seeks assurances from President Obama that this new reporting program will be carried out in a manner consistent with the First Amendment and America's tradition of free speech and public discourse. Cornyn cannot stand this initiative so he asked a number of questions, including:

> *"How do you intend to use the names, email addresses, IP addresses, and identities of citizens who are reported to have engaged in 'fishy' speech and what action do you intend to take against citizens who have been reported for engaging in 'fishy' speech? "*

Students of the Constitution know that The First Amendment states, in part, that Congress shall make no law . . . abridging the freedom of speech, or of the press; or the right of the people peaceably to assemble. The Founding Fathers would not like any private parchments, fishy or not, being turned over to King George or to any member of the government unless a citizen offered them willingly.

Ironically, President Obama campaigned on the promise of a more transparent and open government. His new White House reporting program seems aimed at stifling debate on his healthcare takeover plan. While he knows that he cannot ban such speech, causing individuals to have fear of being reported may have the intended effect of stifling dissent. Fear of being reported to the authorities will discourage many naysayer's from speaking out. Are we talking about America here!

It is easy to be concerned that this might be just the beginning as an army of Obamaczars and snitches-in-chief get released upon an unwary public. Will the next step be to take roll at town halls and place double asterisks next to anybody speaking in opposition to healthcare reform or any other presidential initiative? Don't even think about writing an Op Ed piece. And, oh, hide this book someplace. And, if you find me in the gulags someday, offer me a big rope and then the two of us can run like hell. Thanks!

Sources: My thanks to JB Williams article titled Obamanomics 101 For Useful Idiots, September 11, 2008
http://www.canadafreepress.com/index.php/article/4966

The Neal Boortz Commencement Speech
http://boortz.com/more/commencement.html

Chapter 8   Sin # 6 of 7. Cap & Trade

SneakyPetes Live In Congress

On June 26, 2009, a bit before the sneakypetes that we elect to the House of Representatives took their summer break, they snuck through the infamous Carbon Cap and Trade bill. Most Americans, I fear, are unaware of the full meaning of this bill. Unlike the clear issues involved with the bill they are creating to take away our private health insurance, this does not appear to affect anybody in such a way. It does.

Surely our trustworthy Congress would not put a sneakypete title on a sneakypete bill if it were important and then sneak away for a summer break. But this is what they did. The heated healthcare insurance discussion gave them the cover they needed to not be confronted.

This bill had been debated from May 20, first in the Energy and Commerce Committee and later in the full House. Once they started debate, the essence of what the bill contains was right on the table for all to see, and none of it was good for John Q. Public. There was a lot of income enhancement opportunity for former Vice President Al Gore, but the advantages to anybody other than government, after private citizen Gore got his, could not be found even by straining the bill with a nit comb.

Polluters, Go to the Back of the Line

The bill is designed to create a "cap-and-trade" system that forces polluters to amass credits equal to their emissions. Hidden in the language of the bill, all Americans are declared polluters. If you have enjoyed 70 degree air conditioned temperatures indoors in the summer when the outside temperature was 72, you are a polluter. If you have enjoyed 70 degree temperatures indoors in the winter when the outdoor temperature was 68 degrees, you are a polluter.

If you have ever turned on a light, you are a polluter. If you drive a car, you are a polluter. If you are awakened each morning by a clock of sorts powered by anything other than a wind-up key, you are a polluter. If you have ever had food last for more than a month, when the outside temperature was over 32 degrees Fahrenheit, you are a polluter. Do I have to continue? Remove all the "ifs, ands, and buts," you are a polluter.

The good news; however, is that all Americans will not have to pay this tax. The tax will be born only by polluters.

Well, that explains cap and trade, don't you think? Me neither! It would seem that regardless of the clarity of the "cap and trade" system to be created, the bill seems to apply only to polluters and thus you and I should have nothing to worry about. Unfortunately, like it or not, you are a polluter and I am a polluter according to the Bill - sorry!

Since the Bill Did Not Pass Why Is CAP 'n Trade In this Book?

This remains as sin#6 in this second edition because it is serious big time. Moreover, it is such a contrivance that it is hard to believe that grown-up human beings would put together such a convoluted piece of claptrap so that their cronies would benefit from something supposedly designed to help the people. The people would pay and Obama and Al Gore cronies would get rich.

Al Gore of course would be able to get even richer than the Clintons on Global Warming. Gore left the White House with $2 million and now has $300 million. The Clintons say they left broke but had borrowed White House furniture and Silverware in their asset Cush, and now are worth over $100 million so looks like Gore wins. Who really knows?

It is in this book because we all need to know what cap 'n trade is as even without Obama, the Democrats are likely to try this trick again.

Bill with Amendments to Amendments

Just like most legislation these days, this 1,428 page, $846 billion law was rammed through the house with little time for the representatives to read it. They saw the bill for the first time 16.5 hours before voting on it. But that did not stop them. Nancy said they had to vote on it. Nancy Pelosi, a person who nobody knew just a year ago, who is very important because she is the House Leader, insisted the vote be done before even a full day had passed. To make matters worse, Pelosi squeezed in a 300 page amendment to the bill (included in page count above). Why an eleventh hour 300 page amendment? The only answer I can come up with is that probably some friend of a friend was excluded from making their millions from the wake of the bill.

Hurry Hurry Hurry

Obviously, there was no real time to debate it and no real time to read the bill or the amendment. Shame on Congress! Shame! Shame! Shame! But, it's OK because the devil made them do it. Well, maybe it was not the devil, but it was the President and it was the Pelosi. They pushed this thing through as fast as a Ryne Duren fastball (1954 to 1965 - Yankees) would create an HBP stat.

One day after President Obama made an urgent and impassioned plea for congressional approval in what could have been a make-or-break test of his young administration, Congress voted it in. "Now is the time for us to lead," Obama said during his speech in the White House Rose Garden. He continued, "We cannot be afraid of the future. We cannot be prisoners to the past." He did not say that American citizens could not afford the bill, but every analysis that I have seen suggests that to be the case. Why? It's simple, "Yes, Virginia, there are polluters and we are them."

In all fairness, those on the Energy committee did debate the bill, but not the full House. Make no bones about this, it is really groundbreaking and for the American taxpayer, it is backbreaking legislation to supposedly control US greenhouse gas emissions. Surprise, there is no real evidence this will work. Moreover, many economists suggest in addition to everything else, the bill is economy-breaking. Mmm mmm mm, Barack Hussein Obama and Nancy Pelosi are the only ones I ever heard about who would be so unwise as to break an already broken economy.

What Really is Cap and Trade?

The cap and trade essence again, hard to explain, is to set in motion a new, clean-energy economy using a notion labeled "cap and trade." This "greenhouse gas solution" is purported to provide the certainty that reductions will be achieved by setting emissions goals or caps. It also assures that the goals can be reached through the creation of what are called tradable permits. In other words, if your company is deemed a polluter, you can trade something of value, such as a huge sum of money to buy the rights to continue polluting, from someone who has become green and has extra carbon credits to spare.

Can you imagine the bureaucracy needed to handle this? But, don't worry, the government will be fair. By the way, this is what might be called the government controlled option for energy. Private industry need not apply. Energy production and use will never be the same after cap and trade. It will affect consumers initially as a simple energy tax. Simple to say but very hard to pay -- well over $1000 and approaching $200 for each household per year forever and after forever, it will probably cost lots more. And that $4.00 per gallon gas you thought was in the past, how about $5.00?

What Do Regular Americans Think Of Cap and Trade?

Sometimes, the best way to introduce a notion is to show what folks are thinking about it. So, I collected these posts from the Internet and removed the names to protect the innocent. If anybody finds their quote here, let me know and I would be glad to put your name on our Web site if you so desire. These numbered posts are random and are from various Internet blogs.

1. For example, if you need to run your A/C because you have asthma, then you will be charged so much, you will not be able to buy your medicine. Oh, wait. That will be taken care of with the new Health Care System. The new Govt. Health Care plan will not allow a doctor to treat someone unless it will IMPROVE their health. Oooops, asthmatics won't improve, their treatments are only for maintenance. As with diabetics, AIDS patients, children with CF, CS, MS, Jerry's kids, and on and on and on. Oh, wait. I get it. THAT will reduce energy AND medical costs, as people disappear from the planet -- well, after the obligatory decomposition phase.

2. First, global warming is not proven science, it is far from it. Why is every scientist that has facts or a differing opinion shunned by the media, and blacklisted from science all together? Let's look at the big picture. I can understand people want to do good for the environment but everyone is missing the big point. Global Warming (now global climate change) is a HUGE BUSINESS!!!! All this equates to is a money making machine.

Let me explain the typical American. Go to work, come home read the news and see "Global Warming" everywhere, basically the media has made this a SCIENTIFIC FACT when in reality it is not. No American will do their homework so they go right along with it. If the news says it then it is fact. (channel change to American idol now).

Why don't they have a prime time show with scientists on both sides of the aisle to debate this for the common American to see? Think of all the money these scientists get from the government to slant their studies so that the gov. can throw a fat tax on you. Step outside your political party box and look real hard at what is going on people. Do some research, put the big mac and tv remote down and stimulate your brain.

3. I agree that this whole GLOBAL WARMING I mean CLIMATE CHANGE is a sham. I have heard that there are over a hundred Climatologists who are opposed to this pop-cultural phenomenon, but can't get any media time. And I agree that it is all about $$$. Obama and the UN are using this to

implement Cap and Trade and that stupid Carbon Tax.
Crooks!

Anyway, this Climate Change thing reminds me of that whole
USA for Africa fiasco. Remember that? My High School
worked for weeks raising relief money. It wasn't until later we
found out that it all went to waste. Where is my oversized white
sweatshirt?

4. Why are you people so willing to be controlled by the federal
government? It is no surprise that the Democrats who claim
man is causing global warming are now finding a way to tax
you and control your behavior... Wake up people the next
thing you know they will be taxing the amount of air your
breath.

I'm not advocating polluting our air, or our oceans but being
taxed for the amount of Carbon we use? Are you kidding me?
The number one green house gas is water vapor and it omits
99.46% of the total Co2 into the atmosphere. Even if what the
liberal left is telling you is true that we are causing climate
change there is no way for us to stop water vapor and even if we
stop everything we do that is just a small portion of the Co2
that is going into the atmosphere (.0054%)

Slowly but surely all of our God given rights are being stripped.
America needs to wake up and discover that this whole man
made global warming thing is a complete and utter hoax.

The earth has survived millions of years of natural disasters,
thousands of volcanoes and earthquakes, thousands of tsunami's
and tornadoes. endless hurricanes... And then man who has in
the past 60 or 70 years of the industrial revolution has caused
the planet to heat up? Really??

5. *It certainly is hard to imagine how naive the American people have become. I am blown out of the water at how easy people jump on the band wagon without knowing the real facts. It seems like we will destroy ourselves without any natural disaster. I do believe that a revolution will occur some years from now. Too bad it will be too late! Our government is going to sink us!*

6. *Sadly, many of the mainstream proponents of "Global Warming" live much more lavishly than the everyday American. They have huge homes with fancy amenities that require large amounts of electricity. However, they can ease their conscious by purchasing carbon credits and donating to causes and non-profits that advocate green living. I don't see Al Gore driving across the county in a Prius to make his speaking engagements. At the very least, he could fly commercial. Is a private Jet necessary? What about the so-called "green" inauguration where hundreds of thousands of people showed up to celebrate the most liberal president in history? They acted like the entire event was "green", however, the "green" thing to do would to have NOT had the event AT ALL! Air it out over the TV and encourage people to stay home. That would have been the responsible thing to instead of having people drive and fly from all over the country thereby creating more pollution. But no, the whole climate change theory and "green living" is only a ploy to control average people and profit in the process. I wish we had politicians who would stand up for us who aren't buying into the lies.*

7. *... you are so right. That is one reason Bush thankfully did not sign the Kyoto Treaty. It favored only the developing nation and punished us until they caught up with us economically. Of course no one in their right mind would want the US to continue to be the only super power. If we continue our direction*

it might solve our illegal immigrant problem [Cap and Trade] as who will want to come here to improve their lives?

8. Don't you think Cap and Trade can be viewed as the ultimate tax, where governments can tax life itself by taxing either the intake or by-product of all living things?

They're trying to tax breathing!!!

Your incentive now will be to breathe less, and the only way to avoid this tax is not to be alive.

Since when has CO2 become a pollutant? Plants take in CO2 in day to breathe (so plants need pollution to stay alive?).

9. If the US completely removed all the carbon emissions from our utility industry, we would have only removed approximately 8% of the WORLD'S carbon emissions. Meanwhile we have driven the cost of electricity to a point that only the wealthy can afford it. China is currently adding one new coal fired power plant on per week with none of the clean air controls that our coal power plants currently have. Does it really work if you only clean one corner of the pool?

Will China's excessive pollution not eventually drift our way?

If we drive the cost of electricity up 30%, 40% or 50% or more this will affect the cost of groceries, clothing, etc. Big manufacturing jobs will once again look for locations in China and India where the utility bill alone doesn't eat up all of their profit.
Clean air needs to be a priority, but Cap and Trade is not the answer.

10. There is big evidence that the planet earth is cooling. Carbon will not destroy this planet. It will do it on it's own. If you reduce carbon dioxide the trees and plants don't breathe, therefore we don't get the oxygen we need. Why junk scientists can't get this through their heads is a both a conundrum and an enigma, as well as a puzzle.

11. Cap and trade? A made-up money grubbing scam. First a complete moron comes along with a stupid "theory" about "global warming." After a while, this isn't playing well, because the atmospheric scientist have his freaking number. The "warmers", or the followers of this phony Pied Piper, change the name to "climate change." Their thinking is that by changing the name, they won't have to explain why it isn't getting "warmer." The stupid continue to follow and the low level swine politicos smell money, so it persists. Just as Hitler once said, "If we tell a lie often enough, soon everyone will believe it."

Anyone who is stupid enough to buy into this crap, I have a real nice bridge in NY that I will let go real cheap!

End of Internet posts

What Does the Wall Street Journal Think?

The Wall Street Journal is a very prestigious business publication in the US that has been printed continuously since being founded on July 8, 1889, by Charles Dow, Edward Jones, and Charles Bergstresser. The WSJ, as it is often referenced, can smell whether something is bad for business and bad for Americans. WSJ has big problems with cap and trade. Just because it is good for the greenest millionaire, Al Gore, does not mean it is good for you or I or even the planet

According to WSJ, "cap and trade is the tax that dare not speak its name." It is by any other name an energy tax with enough complications to assure the creation of a huge bureaucracy and more government than anybody needs in their lives.

The hard left and the go along to get along Democrats are all for this legislation (perhaps all Dems but me). They are hoping, in particular, that you and I do not notice who is going to pay for their "green" climate ambitions. This bill is pro grass, pro tree, pro smelt, pro endangered species, but unfortunately, it is not pro human, or as once we were able to say, it is anti-man.

Let Trees Have Better, More Fulfilling Lives

Cass Sunstein thinks humans are no better than the rest of the animals, so maybe this is the thinking that drives cap and trade. The objective is that in order to give the trees a more fulfilling and better life, those nasty polluting humans will have to make the sacrifices. With the coldest summer on record just past us in 2009, Al Gore and the greenies still want us to believe that the earth is warming and everything is melting.

Under any circumstances, let my position clear. If anybody has to suffer, let it be the trees. Sorry Cass. By the way, the name change of "global warming" to "climate change" is very clever now that the evidence is in that the earth is actually cooling. What do the computer models say about that?

I don't buy it, just like I don't buy that illegal aliens were not included in healthcare legislation before Joe Wilson, the world's favorite "liar" called them out. Cap and trade, as it is called, is all about giving President Obama, who is depending on vast new carbon tax revenues in his budget, the opportunity to deliver his promises to the hard left. Do you think that Obama cares if your 401k has any value? Do you think Obama cares if you can't get a job because less carbon is being emitted? Congress is very complicit and had promised to deliver this bill to the President by

May, but even with Obama's call to hurry, hurry, hurry before it is too late, they could not get it done. And, Harry did not get it done at all.

Who Pays?

When you really look at this, you may wonder who will pay for it. When Congress and the President spend more than we have, they have to get more from us or from the Chinese, who long ago decided not to pay homage to the US. So, Virginia, the answer to who is going to pay for this huge revenue bonanza is me and you when you are older, and your children and their children....

Unless an American such as yourself decides to turn off the heat, ladies and gentlemen, you and I have been labeled as the big polluters caught by this big bill by Obama's czar-protected big government. Get ready to pay up when the Tax-Man cometh. He is on the doorstep. It won't be fun. Mmm mmm mm Barack Hussein Obama. I can't get that tune out of my mind.

It Ain't Just Me Babe!

To get the details of any cap and trade theory, there are lots of sources on the Internet. Just enter the term cap and trade into your favorite search engine. Be aware that most of the sources explain the notion in very positive terms, and not in terms of how the notion is to be implemented if the Senate subsumes to the will of Obama. The Internet folks typically provide the hard left description of how the cap and trade scheme works and how they see its effects being very positive for the environment. There is no concern about all Americans heading for the "poor house." There is no concern about Americans finding the "poor house" filled. Then what?

They do not discuss the human cost in most cases, so be wary. Actually if we were all willing not to drive and not to travel on airplanes, and not turn on the heat all winter, we would know who was doing the capping and who was doing the trading and who was doing the suffering. By the way, while you are freezing next winter, don't think of turning on your TV or computer for a bit of enjoyment as that too adds to your personal carbon burden.

Smart Grid Snitches

Hard left ideas get even worse over time. You may know that the government and electric companies are working on the "smart grid" to deliver electricity smartly. Hah! This grid can not only give you power, but through the same or similar wires, it can receive input from your house and it can control devices in your house.

Maybe you already have the devices, but once the "smart grid" is operational, Rod Serling and Walt Disney will be defrosted and you will swear you are either in the Twilight Zone or in Disney's Haunted House, which will be cold, by the way -- unless it is the summer.

Though I joke, this is not joke. In other words, the government computers will be able to monitor the appliances you are using in your home and if you are taking more than your share of power, a government worker named Clarence will get a computer generated text message. Now, Clarence wants to get home early every day so he is not about to call you before he shuts off your power. You see, Clarence is a "Microsoft Certified Green Guy." He wants you to use no power so the trees and the smelts have a good day. Unless Clarence turns a different knob, and he is trying to get home early, you will be automatically capped, so you won't even need a thermostat. Because you are just you, there will be no trading for more. Now you know what cap means. Clarence has no control of daylight so you can be assured your day will have more daylight in the summer. Thanks Clarence.

More People, More Credits

In a fair plan, those in residences that have many people should be able to get more credits in total for heat as long as the people are registered with the power company. Today when you want more power, you take it and they bill you and you pay -- sometimes through the nose. Those days are gone, no matter how big your nose. You can't even pay for it with the smart grid.

Please Kind Sir, Grant Me More Power?

In the future, you can lay humbly prostrate before a powerful bureaucrat and plead your case to have more power. With Cass Sunstein in the White House, if you have a dog or a cat, and they can reach the Cassmeister, you have a good chance of getting that power boost... if the dog or the cat make your case well enough. If you are selfish, living alone in a nice pad that is paid for and you expect to heat that sucker all winter, think again.

I am not doing any equating here, but there are those in the administration that also might give you credit if you have a number of illegal aliens benefiting from the heat. There will probably be a form you can fill out for extra credit. Your own children would not count, of course, unless they were of productive age -- from 15 to 40, according to Sunstein.

Maybe I am stretching a bit, but the point is you will be kissing your freedom goodbye for each kilowatt you consume. The only other kissing option comes when you see your friendly energy bureaucrat. By the way, the lipstick from the many kisses before yours would not be seen on this impresario's face.

Please Give Congress A Better Deal

The good news is while you are sweating in the summer and freezing in the winter, you will not have to worry about the person who represents you in Congress. They are so important that they will have their own energy plan. No matter how bad anybody ever thought George Bush was, and he was bad in many ways, his worst idea was better than this.

Maybe we need to check the czar list again because this whole cap and trade nonsense is one of the worse scripts I have ever read even though it appears to have been written by Rod Serling and Walt Disney. Perhaps more and more will want to visit the Twilight Zone or Disney World after living a few years in the new Obama world. Hopefully, the wind powered green car will be available then.

How about a car powered by body emissions. Then, everybody would be trying to get everybody else to go on vacations with them in the little green machine. Many a true word is said in jest.

Mmm mmm mm Yeah Obama

It might help you as you are trying to figure out whether this is good or bad to remember that it is always a socialist trick to get individuals to cheer for the big government team. In the euphoria, you are more willing to permit government into your private life and you might also accept higher taxes if you live differently than Uncle Sam prescribes.

But, what if there is no choice and there are no higher taxes? What if you will have to comply? If you think this is about to affect your freedom and your choices, you are leaving this Chapter with the right message.

Pay Your Fair Share of Pollution

Of course, the energy tax or the "climate costs" will be distributed equally just like the government controlled healthcare option will make sure you are still living while others are dying. No discrimination will be made across regions and income groups. As noted, government officials have a different energy plan so they will be just fine. Remember, this is the government energy option you are getting and everybody gets it. Cap and trade is just a euphemism for energy tax, but so what if it is for the state.

If this is exactly what you and I do not want, you might check the archives, since the House of Representatives already passed the bill on June 26. They are waiting for the laggards in the Senate to get the rest of the work done. Give your Senator a call.

Politicians really love this deal because it enables them to single you out as a polluter and it gives them a right to grab more of your income because of the sin of pollution, while they, of course, are exempt. Of course, they never say it is you who will pay. It is those nasty polluters. Once our representatives give the government the right to treat energy as a scarce new commodity -- in other words, once you need permission to use energy and you need the government's permission to emit carbon, a natural effect of using energy of any kind, you are now indebted to the government to let you use energy -- whether you can afford it or not.

Perhaps before the "smart grids," they can create neighborhood energy czars who can check your power meters every day and advise you of your options. Let's suggest that to the Administration and maybe we can get some energy favors, like an extra kilowatt every now and then.

Big Businesses Have Big Advantages

Additionally, in the cap and trade legislation that passed the house, the government mandates that businesses buy the credits just to be able to use any power and you know that the costs of the energy credits are going to be exorbitant. This is from whence your tax is calculated. If you are able to get permission to use energy, then you get to pay your share of the cost of the tax credit that the coal or electric or gas company paid to the government, allowing of course for a profit for the company, even on the credits themselves.

So we are clear, all of this is passed on to all consumers in the form of higher prices. Don't think that Obama and your congressman do not know this already. In fact, they are counting on it to bring in mucho revenue. Peter Orszag, who at the time of this writing is Mr. Obama's Budget Director, told Congress last year that "Those price increases are essential to the success of a cap-and-trade program."

Mikey Moore Speaks Up

Michael Moore, in a 2009 interview with Rolling Stone, which I read intently, gave away the Obama strategy regarding dealing with the people and dealing with the opposition (Republicans) on any of his programs. Moore used a basketball analogy. Before my editor chopped it from a prior section, I had discussed this analogy earlier in this book. Even if Melissa L. Sabol puts it back in the earlier section, It bears repeating.

Moore noted in the analogy how well Obama plays basketball. His words were that Obama basically says what people want to hear. That is how he wins. According to Moore, Obama "fakes right and goes left." The notions, right and left, are exactly what we have seen so far.

No Taxes?

Do you remember the President, during the campaign or in the early 2009 Energy Tax negotiations, talking about a huge energy tax that will cost middle class families as much as $3,000 if you pay for heating your home (on top of the heating bill)? If on the other hand, somebody else pays for the heat, your tax increase for energy may be in the neighborhood of $1,000.00 per year.

He must have forgotten to tell us. You see, when Congress raises taxes on your suppliers of energy or of dental floss, they increase their prices to you. So, you don't see it as a tax unless the company chooses to mark the government's share someplace on the bill. Like me, you are looking at what you have to pay, not why the price is so high. Just get your wallet out.

Who pays the bill? Answer: Everybody pays. However, the people that will be hardest hit are going to be the "95% of working families." Don't forget, there is an Energy Czar to assure compliance. The Energy Czar will work with your friends in the IRS to assure you do not lie. Lying is for government only. Lie # 1 on Energy is that when President Obama continually mentions his no-new-taxes pledge he means that sincerely. However as an incentive to use no energy, Obama's pledge is good "unless you use energy."

So that you and I are more easily duped into believing that the "Energy Tax" is not a tax, we will be asked to pay it to the Electric Company, the Gas Company, or the Gas Station. It won't seem that the government raised taxes. Meanwhile to pay the carbon tax, our legislators will need an increase in their personal driving allowances as a "carbon offset." The poor and middle-income households will spend lots more of their paychecks on things like gas to drive to work, groceries or home heating. Unlike Congressman X and, of course, the typical working class citizens have no driving allowances, so this thing is going to hurt. It is going to hurt us all.

Bad for Business Is Bad for America?

The Wall Street Journal is a great paper. It is fact oriented with few opinions. Their opinion slants them against this legislation because it is bad for business. That is not an opinion, it is a fact. It will cost lots of jobs as businesses move jobs to China and elsewhere since they have no energy tax. The Chinese are laughing at Obama and all of America. Mahmoud Ahmadinejad can even outfox Obama's America. We are an international joke.

Cap and trade is also bad for consumers and anybody wanting to hold a job -- ever. The WSJ's concluding remarks in a 2009 article about cap and trade are given below. It's nice to have somebody on our side as our representatives surely are not: You do know how to solve that one, don't you?

"An economy-wide tax under the cover of saving the environment is the best political moneymaker since the income tax. Obama officials are already telling the press, sotto voce, that climate revenues might fund universal health care and other new social spending. [Hello Government Control, Bye Bye Freedom]. No doubt they would, and when they did Mr. Obama's cap-and-trade rebates would become even smaller.

Cap and trade, in other words, is a scheme to redistribute income and wealth -- but in a very curious way. It takes from the working class and gives to the affluent; takes from Miami, Ohio, and gives to Miami, Florida; and takes from an industrial America that is already struggling and gives to rich Silicon Valley and Wall Street "green tech" investors who know how to leverage the political class."

And for what? So Al Gore can buy another plane and add to his $100 million bonanza. Would that be an inconvenient truth? Do you want big government controlling all aspects of your life? Forget about writing your congressman. It does not work. Show up at their doorsteps if you can get the keys to enter their gated communities. In 2010, make sure you show up to vote and vote for the wall rather than these ... you know!

That's that!

Cap and trade was rejected by the American people but Obam is still in love with the idea.

Nobody is in favor of pollution, especially conservative democrats but I will bet a dollar to a donut that the big six, in the wanted posters, poised to benefit from the Waxman legislation have polluted more than all the 2 million people at the freedom rally in Washington DC on September 12, 2009. Yet, because they line up with the right team (leftward leaning), they are rewarded.

Dear Government, What's the hurry? Why can't we see if this legislation has merit? If it were so good, would China not be doing the same thing? The Chinese are using capitalism to beat an America headed for socialism.

Whodathunk? China and the other big polluters across the globe are not going to punish their people to save the minnow smelt or the malaria causing one wing cross eyed mosquito. Why should we? Why is Obama screaming NOW NOW NOW, and why are the kids chanting, mmm mmm mm? Why are there no questions permitted? Why don't our representatives read the 1500 page bill?

Why don't they represent us instead of representing Jeffrey Immelt and why don't they "just say no!" We hope that there are some smart people left in the Senate.

Can we all agree that any step taken to fix a non-existent problem would be by definition, unreasonable, no matter how small it is. So, if this tax on carbon were not so big, but instead just cost each of us say $5 bucks a year, it still would only be reasonable if global warming is real. The real science refutes global warming / climate change. The truth lies in what those smart greenhouse gas scientists are saying. Being a computer guy, with lots of experience, I don't trust computer models with good input without good testing and I surely do not trust computer models with divined input from a bunch of freaks with an agenda. The whole deal is a lie and so any step taken, no matter how small, to fix it, is clearly unreasonable.

So, let's all say No, Loud and clear to the Waxman Crap and Tax bill. Make sure all the Congress people -- in both houses know that we are very displeased with them. I think they already know it but let's tell them again anyway. Say it again Sam!

And, also, let's tell them after 2010, we do not plan to tell them again.

Chapter 9   Sin 7 of 7. Obamacare -- the Big Item – The Big Failure!

The hard fought, blood drenched American Democracy Experiment that was begun by our forefathers is in danger of an early demise. While we are all hoping healthcare in the US can be reformed, our democracy needs a visit to a doctor who practices founding father type medicine. The change Americans asked for on November 4, 2008 has arrived with a powerful force that is much further reaching than anyone, optimist or pessimist, could have imagined.

The world for Americans began to change swiftly, even before January 20, 2009, the day Barack Hussein Obama was inaugurated President of the US. Instead of a patient upper and lower House, and an Administration wanting to get its feet a little wet before mixing up a huge batch of change, anything in America became fair game, and everything became an emergency. And it started almost from the minute the last vote was tallied in November.

Obama's team clearly intended to hit the ground running in January 2009. They did and the American people have observed the chaos presented by an ideologue ever since. Maybe the administration was over-prepared. Maybe the essence of the change offered was not the essence of the change that was delivered.

There was an immediate wild frenzy to pass huge bills, read or not, high impact or not. Many Americans read this as the government not wanting the people to know what was in the legislation before the bills were passed. Everything was a crisis and the reaction to the crisis, has, in fact, created a crisis for America of possibly epic proportions.

Healthcare has been embroiled as part of that feeling of crisis. Universal Healthcare and Single Payer Options took center stage in mid-2009 while jobs were being lost by the droves. Why not get the public back to work first? What's the rush when 85% of Americans are happy with their current methodology -- not that it cannot be made better.

Obama, Pelosi, Reid Style

It's the Obama, Pelosi, Reid style, but it is not helpful to America or Americans. Bills were presented as crisis solutions without crises being declared. The congressional modus operandi was to fully eliminate the Republican voice from making amendments and then call for a vote. Poof! Like magic, big new laws were on the books. The year 2009 was an absolute sham of partisan politics from a guy who promised to work for good changes for all the people—not just the hard left.

The Bogeyman was Coming and He Arrived!

To assure that the laws were passed, the crisis atmosphere always brought in the threat of the Bogeyman ruining American lives, if the bills were not passed. At first Americans believed it since nobody wanted the big bad Bogeyman to ruin the country. It was not too long into months of the two-minute drill that Americans got sick of the reckless spending, the pork and the uttermost disdain for public opinion. In retrospect, it was the lousy legislation and not the Bogeyman that anybody had to worry about.

Congress "worked so hard" that they had no time even to read most, if not all, of these emergency bills that we covered in great detail in the prior chapters. In March 2009, after just a few Obama months, Kevin Jackson of the BlackSphere rightfully predicted a crash of Obama's politics and he noted what he thought was the old Bogeyman that was forcing Obama and company to push out their legislation so quickly.

"Obama has tried to revive the ghost of the Boogeyman, which is 'eight years of George Bush'...you know, that mean old White racist Republican, who could be blamed for everything under the sun. However the tread is wearing off those tires with each drop in the stock market. I ain't 'fraid of no ghosts... Ghostbusters!"

In the spirit of Kevin Jackson's humor, can't you see little Stevey Urkel, shown in Figure 9-1, taking on all of America's problems, solving them, and putting his hands on his hips without saying a word. Urkel was afraid of no ghosts.

Figure 9-1 Jaleel White as the Real Steve Urkel

Jackson ends his blog by offering an idea about who the new Bogeyman is for America, and it is not Steve Urkel shown above. It is more like the new Urkel, shown from Jackson's site in the below picture. Note the major resemblance that Jackson clearly finds amusing, and quite frankly, so do I. Did I do that? Yes, you did Mr. President, you did that. Please take a few days off. Jackson knows who the real Bogeyman is as he wraps up his Ghostbusters soliloquy:

"And by the way America, I'd like to introduce you to the new and real Bogeyman...Barack Hussein Obama."

Figure 9-2 From www.blacksphere.com home page

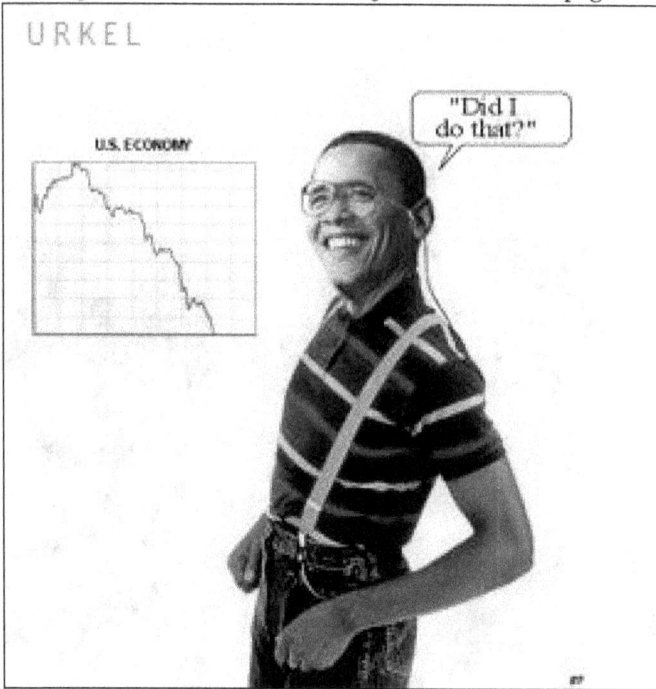

The Health debate began after folks like Jackson and many other concerned Americans across the country already began to feel the President melting down. But he is so stubborn and so convinced that he is the grand difference maker that you can expect no back-tracking, even if he is way wrong.

One of the ironies of this healthcare debate, which is the focus of this chapter, is that unlike many Presidents before him, Obama's White House did not write the health bill(s). Thus, even the

President cannot know what is in each and every version of every healthcare bill that was floating in the House and the Senate for most of 2009. Yet, I am convinced, based on my profile of the man that he would insist that he does know. Though I am not inside his head, but I am working on it, I am convinced he could pass a lie detector test on that.

Obviously, we the people have no real opportunity to know the contents of the bills, but we know and freely admit that we don't know. Five bills were being debated in the Senate and the House. In late 2009, there was the Reid bill and the Pelosi bill which replaced all five.

Despite all this prose in either legislative language, in outline form or in markup form, the majority of Americans has said thanks, but no thanks, to one and all bills coming from the perverted process. The message is that Americans do not want the government involved in their healthcare. Moreover, Americans do not want the government to control any aspect of the healthcare industry or the healthcare insurance industry. Thanks again, but no thanks.

There was a time much later in the Clinton Administration when a bad case of "Clinton fatigue." had set in. The glitter and the enamor of Slick Willie, the Comeback Kid, dimmed as the years went by. This book is not a slam on Democrats. Bill Clinton was the finest orator I had ever seen, even greater than Ronald Reagan, though with less substance. Over time, he could not contain the corruption that surrounded his Administration. Americans grew fatigued with the excuses and got sick of both Clintons for a while.

There is this notion of corruption and a politician, such as Bill Clinton, and now Hillary Clinton, that fits this quote voiced by an early American patriot and hero, Thomas Paine:

"It is impossible to calculate the moral mischief, if I may so express it, that menial lying has produced in society. When a man has so far corrupted and prostituted the chastity of his mind as to subscribe his professional belief to things he does not believe, he has prepared himself for the commission of every other crime."

I don't see the fatigue with Obama in the same light but I am beginning to see fatigue, nonetheless. I have been having Obama for breakfast, supper, and a midnight snack, and that is far too much Obama TV for my digestive tract to handle. Though it is still early, I am getting that same feeling as with the Clintons, Perhaps many like me are suffering from Obama fatigue. I hope so because with Hillary clinton, the fatigue will continue.

If I actually believed in anything Obama has done, which of course Hillary Clinton would swear is the best, it would be easier for me to take in the message. Please do not suggest that the only remedy for my Obama fatigue is huge dosage of government controlled Obamacare. If I could make a hair-pulling-out sound now, I would.

It seems that after having all kinds of bad stuff rammed down our throats from January 20, 2009 onwards, the US citizenry, Democrat, Republican, both Black, and White, have quietly banded together from the August 2009 break on, to deliver a loud and clear message that we wanted none of what Obama and the Congress were serving up. Yet it did not matter to them.

What became of the five health bills? The Senate Finance bill was doctored up by Senator Max Baucus so much that for a while it bore his name. It was merged with the Senate Health Committee bill after the CBO (Congressional Budget Office) scored it at somewhat less than $900 billion. Near the end of 2009, it was the Reid bill. The House had three bills in the works from various committees and On October 28, Nancy Pelosi out of nowhere had the "merged" bill ready to go. It was "only" 1900 pages.

There was speculation rampant that there would be a special maneuver by the Senate Leader Harry Reid that would cut off debate and sneak a bill through that was written by the Leader himself (with staff assistance, of course). The Reid bill was to contain the dreaded "public option" which would put the government in the healthcare business big time, and upset a lot of voters. By the end of October, after many closed door sessions with Rahm Emanuel, the Reid bill did emerge with minimal fanfare.

The Government's goal of controlling the people by controlling industry and by controlling healthcare was not what people wanted. They got the message out loud and clear in the summer 2009, but Harry Reid, Nancy Pelosi, and the President himself, rather than listen to Americans, chose instead to deride the American people and whisper among themselves that "this too shall pass." They decided to make a calculated gamble that they could get elected without the kind of citizens, who would come out to a Town Hall Meeting in an expression of free speech.

The people were upset at the stubbornness of their government leaders. In a united voice, in tea parties and in town halls, people from all over America joined to say no to cap and trade, tax and spend, and government owned healthcare. Reid and Pelosi told the people's representatives to ignore the cry of the folks and go along with another set of "ram it down their throats legislation. This was remembered.

The bill that everybody was looking at, until the Nancy Pelosi bill in October, was the 1017 page Obama healthcare reform bill that came from the House in the summer 2009. We have already discussed the "Baucus Bill." As happy as Senator Baucus was at first about his bill, it was shot down, but then emerged again as one of the standard bearers and was scored by CBO. Then, of course it was replaced by the Reid bill.

One of the reasons the Baucus Bill was unloved by Democrats originally was that it was contrary to the principles of campaign payback to Unions. You see, Union members with Cadillac insurance plans -- nothing like yours and mine, would have to pay tax on those plans. It would be kind of like our deductibles and copays that we have in our plans.

The Unions gave a big "no" to that and their minions in Congress echoed their "no." to Max Baucus. But, Baucus got up, dusted himself off and got a new bill out. Reid then took his bill and the HELP bill from the Senate and merged them into his own bill.

What is in the Obamacare Bill?

One of the best synopses of the summer bill and one of the shortest was found on the Internet. The October Pelosi bill had similar language but a lot more of it. An apparent "Army Translator" was found who was able to speak both "Weasel," the newly adopted language of the House, though remarkably it is also spoken by Senator Casey from my home state of PA and also "Washington Doublespeak."

Both skills were necessary for this military career gentleman to possess (fluent weasel and doublespeak), I suspect to do such a fine job. His translation in plain-language without any of my extra annotations can be found at FreeRepublic.com (http://www.freerepublic.com/focus/f...).

We have taken the liberty to list his English translation of the "proposed health care reform bill," from summer 2009 below. Nobody is perfect and as anybody would translate such a monstrosity of 1017 pages to about 1 page, there is some room for interpretation and extrapolation. The risk for me is that you may not buy it all but it is cause for concern if it is half right. The exact translation as noted above is at the Web site listed above. In my own version below, I use the translation as a basis and then further describe what is being said.

From *CMS at FreeRepublic.com*, In Page number sequence:

• **Page 16:** States that if you have insurance at the time of the bill becoming law and you change your plan, you will be required to take a similar plan. If that is not available, you will be required to take the government option! -- also since the government is insisting that all private policies add government speak within 1 to 5 years, when such "speak" is added to your policy, it will have changed and you can just about kiss your policy goodbye, as you will have changed it.

• **Page 22**: Mandates audits of all employers that self-insure! What a treat for those who choose to pay their employees' health care.

• **Page 29:** Admission: your health care will be rationed! Despite how many times you heard it is not true, your health care will be rationed. Those on Medicare will be hit hard.

• **Page 30:** A government committee will decide what treatments and benefits you get (and, unlike an insurer, there will be no appeals process to the government,) which ought to make the system more efficient because there will be no time wasted in having to hear us whine about no coverage. Plus, when we die from our government determined, untreated illnesses, there will be more healthcare money left for those who are uninsured today.

• **Page 42**: The "Health Choices Commissioner" will decide health benefits for you. You will have no choice. None. I am sure he or she will be a nice person with the title "CZAR."

• **Page 50:** All non-US citizens, illegal or not, will be provided with free healthcare services, regardless of how many times the President denies it. You will pay by first giving up your own insurance.

• **Page 58**: Every person will be issued a National ID Health card. There is nothing there that says you must be a citizen to get it and if there were, the laws say you do not have to prove citizenship for any reason.

• **Page 59:** The federal government will have direct, real-time access to all individual bank accounts for electronic funds transfer. There is some talk about the IRS managing this to make sure you pay. How about a direct deposit from your account to the IRS at random?

• **Page 65:** Taxpayers will subsidize all union retiree and community organizer health plans (example: SEIU, UAW and ACORN). ACORN is slotted to receive a lot of money. SEIU is the President's own union. ACORN is a bit embattled now so they probably will change their name to make the list.

• **Page 72:** All private healthcare plans must conform to government rules to participate in a Healthcare Exchange. That just about eliminates an insurance company being able to offer a plan similar to which you are accustomed.

• **Page 84:** All private healthcare plans must participate in the Healthcare Exchange (i.e., total government control of private plans.) Whether there is the "public option," which means everybody works for the government or these regulations, one thing is for sure. Freedom of choice is being given up for government control and it will never come back to the people. '

• **Page 91:** Government mandates linguistic infrastructure for services; translation: illegal aliens. This means you don't have to speak English to be covered. I wonder why that is in the bill.

• **Page 95:** The Government will pay ACORN and AmeriCorps to sign up individuals for Government-run Health Care plan. We just can't tell people that their insurance is free via TV and other methods as well as word of mouth, we need the corrupt organization ACORN and others to take our money to find people to sign up. If they are so hard to find, why are we all giving up our healthcare so these folks who can't be found can be covered? Is it so they can catch a quick flight back to the country?

• **Page 102:** Those eligible for Medicaid will be automatically enrolled: you have no choice in the matter.

• **Page 124:** No company can sue the government for price-fixing. No "judicial review" is permitted against the government monopoly. Put simply, private insurers will be crushed. The objective is to begin the "Barry and the Boys" Insurance Company. The President is holding his laughter at the scam he pulled on the American people because he is a smart man. "He who laughs last, laughs best."

• **Page 127:** The AMA sold doctors out: the government will set doctors wages. Other than the 20% doctors in the AMA, real doctors are against the plan.

• **Page 145:** An employer MUST auto-enroll employees into the government-run public plan. No alternatives. Small businesses will drop all employees and let them sign up for the government option. Sorry Charley!

Medicare -- No page references. Since it is very germane to many Americans over 65, President Obama is cutting Medicare by $660 billion dollars. That's by more than 1/2 a trillion. Medicare Advantage will be cut out just about completely so if you are one of the 1 in 3 Seniors who use this method to assure you are OK, kiss it good-by. The man who promised you no changes to your healthcare is taking it away.

Can You Add All That Up?

There are a few cold hearted folks out there who can dance without pain in their knees or hips, and who are doing so well in life that they can't imagine why anybody over 65 should be treated differently than anybody else. I am glad you can dance. As you get older things happen. Your brain still thinks you can dance. You dance. You're then in the ER?

Should that be the end? Unless your parents are aging in front of you and you hear the ughhh—rather than the chair squeak when they get up, you may not think that Senior Citizens deserve as much healthcare as they get. A president taking $500 to $620 billion from Medicare must still be able to play basketball.

Everybody gets old. There are a few facts the young and able bodied people may not fully understand. Senior Citizens under Medicare plans paid into what they had been told was an elderly insurance system. Medicare patients are not getting welfare.

Many dollars were captured for many years from good people's paychecks for today's seniors to now be entitled, by virtue of their Medicare insurance, to have good, if not excellent health care. Doctors of whom I am aware have yet to complain that it is senior citizens overwhelming their practices. Yet, they are quick to assert that the newly covered under Obamacare may put them out of business.

If you want to talk about fair, for all money the seniors paid in, one might think the doctors should get a little more revenue so they could run their practices even better, and they too can have a nice retirement for all the wonderful work they have done saving people's lives.

Something that needs to be known by the young so that they do not begin to resent the old is that there was a system, Social Security and Medicare, two programs introduced by Democrats and passed as law. Everybody contributed to the system up to seven or eight percent of their income and their employers matched giving at least 15% of employee income to health insurance and retirement. Today's retirement insurance plans only ask for 5 or 6 %.

Anyway, I want the young and the able bodied to know that when the old bucks of today were in their twenties or thirties, raising families, they contributed to Social Security and Medicare, from when it was passed 'til now. And, now, it is time for them to collect.

The unfortunate part of all of this is that though the collections came in good faith for health insurance via Medicare, Congress authorized the use of their contributions for other people's needs, or for pet projects, or for things that were illegal and unethical for anybody to do to anybody else. The government collected Social Security and Medicare with good actuarial tables. Then, Congress authorized the government to steal from the fund so that Medicare and Social Security recipients now have no huge pot that is their rainbow, that they can call their own.

This lack of custodianship for seniors' funds is just as bad as the Congress's disregard for our children and our grandchildren and even their children as our debt is so large the Empire State Building is looking up! Can you believe these buffoons in Congress have squandered the contributions of the now elderly so that each American now owes the government $37,000.

Make no bones about it, if you have a dime, Obamacare will be there to collect it. And those Medicare dollars that seniors contributed have all been spent. My point is that the $620 billion that Medicare is having chopped from its budget is not an entitlement. It is paid up insurance.

All of this may not be good enough for Suzi LeVeaux, but it is good enough for me.

To help American Senior Citizens in their fight not to get rammed under the bus as "Grandma" did, Michael Steel, a Republican, took on Obamacare and offered a promise that Republicans would help Seniors Citizens from the wrath of Obama. He called the deal, the Senior Citizens Bill of Rights.

To Suzi LeVeaux, it was a laughing matter, as she was trying to give seniors the best spots under the bus. Suzi doesn't think seniors deserve their healthcare.

On Monday, August 24, 2009 - at 7:40 pm, Suzi LeVeaux got to make her pitch. Most of her pitch was to show how she felt it was for Michael Steele to stick up for seniors. She felt that if seniors would only get out of the way, it would make healthcare for all others more affordable. Age quickly Suzi... Anyway, here are a few paragraphs from the heartless one. I saw more humanity in the Tin Man!

It seems the RNC, with an introduction by Michael Steele, is at it again. With their current unyielding support for senior citizens, they have decided that seniors need their own bill of rights. The Bill of Rights that has served the nation so well isn't enough for the silver set. Oh no, they need protection from the big bad President's vision for health care. So, without further ado, may I present the first and last paragraphs of Mr. Steele's op-ed in the Washington Post, titled "Protecting Our Seniors":

Americans are engaged in a critical debate over reforming our health-care system. While Republicans believe that reforms are necessary, President Obama's plan for a government-run health-care system is the wrong prescription. The Democrats' plan will hurt American families, small businesses and health-care providers by raising care costs, increasing the deficit, and not allowing patients to keep a doctor or insurance plan of their choice. Furthermore, under the Democrats' plan, senior citizens will pay a steeper price and will have their treatment options reduced or rationed.

Barack Obama campaigned on "post-partisanship." As president, however, Obama has shown that he is beholden to his party's left-wing ideologues. It's not too late for him to honor his pledges for bipartisan health-care reform. Reversing course and joining Republicans in support of health care for our nation's senior citizens is a good place to start. Doing so will help him restart the reform process to give Americans access to low-cost, high-quality health care.

Ole Suzi Q explained the words between Michael Steel's two paragraphs as being filled with the usual political spin, misinformation and scare tactics. Suzi offered no explanation for the $620 billion in Medicare cuts. That is a fact, nobody's spin. It's the real deal.

How a benefits cut is good for seniors is something folks like Suzi, perhaps waiting to turn 21 any day, cannot appreciate. Obamacare simply is not good for seniors. Suzi, let me repeat my first set of advice. Don't bother ever getting a heart, but please, "age quickly Suzi."

Americans, listen to Michael Steele who represents honesty and goodness and who tells the truth and then compares that truth with what you have seen coming out of Washington for the past year.

Senior Citizens had better hope that Obama creates an island of unwanted seniors so that along with the unwanted toys, seniors would have some hope, waiting for Santa. For the life of me, I cannot see how Santa could be for anything that would hurt seniors or children. That would mean, of course, that he must not be an Obama supporter. Shhhhh! Santa is not singing, "mmm mmm mm Barack Hussein Obama." Seems like the President is not a believer.

Obamacare wins the day

Obamacare Passed and is now the law of the land. Time pressed on and eventually, the Democrats were able to pass Obamacare.

It was March 23rd, 2010. The Patient Protection and Affordable Care Act, was passed in the Senate on December 24, 2009, and passed in the House on March 21, 2010. It was signed into law by President Obama on March 23rd, 2010 and upheld in the Supreme Court on June 28, 2012. We're stuck with it

A Look Back At How the President Was Able To Sign Obamacare into Law...from www.forbes.com

This post was contributed by Louis J. Goodman, PhD, Board member of the Physicians Foundation and Tim Norbeck, CEO of the Physicians Foundation.

"We have encountered many physicians and friends who don't recall or recognize just how many interesting coincidences had to fall into place for the Affordable Care Act (ACA) to pass both houses of Congress and gain President Obama's signature (March 23, 2010). This post serves as an informational overview – a reminder – as to how it all happened and is not meant in any way to be a judgment on the process – however convoluted – or on the final product.

The U.S. House of Representatives was safely Democratic as a result of the Nov. 4, 2008, elections by a margin of 257 – 199; the Democrats had gained 21 seats from the 2006-07 Congress. The real interesting ACA political dynamics began during the November 2008 U.S. Senate elections.

Going into the 2008 elections, the Senate consisted of 49 Democrats, 49 Republicans, and two Independents (Joe Lieberman of Connecticut and Bernie Sanders of Vermont) who caucused with the Democrats. When the smoke cleared from those elections, the Democrats picked up eight seats to increase their majority to 57-41 (although Democrat Al Franken's recount victory was not official until July 7). With the two Independents, the Democrats were one vote shy of the supermajority magic number of 60 they needed to ward off any filibuster attempts and move forward with broad healthcare reform legislation.

But on April 28, 2009, the dynamics changed when Pennsylvania Republican Arlen Spector changed parties, giving Senate Democrats that coveted 60th vote.

Now the Democrats had a safe majority in the House and a filibuster-proof supermajority of 60 in the Senate. That scenario lasted only four months before fate intervened. Sen. Ted Kennedy of Massachusetts died on August 25, 2009, leaving the Democrats, once again, with 59 seats (counting the two Independents). Exactly one month later, on September 25, Democrat Paul Kirk was appointed interim senator from Massachusetts to serve until the special election set for January 19, 2010 – once again giving the Democrats that 60th vote. But the intrigue was just beginning.

With the supermajority vote safely intact once again, the Senate moved rather quickly to pass the ACA – or ObamaCare – on Christmas Eve 2009 in a 60 – 39 vote (Kentucky Republican Senator Jim Bunning chose not to vote since he was not running for reelection). The House had previously passed a similar, although not identical bill on November 7, 2009, on a 220 – 215 vote. One Republican voted "aye," and 39 Democrats were against.

There didn't seem to be an urgent need for Democrats to reconcile both bills immediately, because the Massachusetts special election (scheduled for January 19, 2010) was almost certain to fall to the Democrat, Attorney General Martha Coakley. After all, no Republican had been elected to the U.S. Senate from the Bay State since Edward Brooke in 1972 – 38 years before! But in yet another twist of fate, Republican Scott Brown ran his campaign as the 41st senator against ObamaCare and shocked nearly everyone by winning the special election by 110,000 votes.

That left House Speaker Nancy Pelosi and President Obama in a dilemma. Everyone assumed that the Christmas Eve 2009 Senate bill would be tweaked considerably to conform more with the House bill passed two months previously. But now that strategy wouldn't work, because the Democrats no longer had the 60th vote in the Senate to end debate. What to do? They decided to have the House take up the identical bill that the Senate passed on Christmas Eve. It passed on March 21, 2010, by a 219 – 212 vote. This time, no Republicans came on board, and 34 Democrats voted against. President Obama signed the ACA legislation two days later on March 23.

The rancor has not abated since, as we all know. Republicans invoked Thomas Jefferson's observation that "great innovations should not be forced on a slender majority – or enacted without broad support." They cited broad legislative innovations like Social Security and Medicare, both of which enjoyed bipartisan support. They complained that one fewer vote in the Senate or a change of four votes in the House would have been enough to defeat ObamaCare. Democrats responded just as vociferously and passionately that this healthcare reform package was too important and overdue to delay or compromise.

We leave it to the readers to form their own opinions, but we felt that the process was a most interesting one – full of coincidences and intrigue that greatly impact what seems to be a never ending discussion and debate on one of the most significant pieces of legislation that the American public has witnessed in many years. So many have forgotten the ACA's legislative genesis, with its many twists of fate and maneuvering, that we thought it would be fascinating to share with you as the continuing commentary goes on. And on. And on."

Chapter 10 Sin # 7 -- Obamacare-- No Free Lunch

Teddy Roosevelt Wanted Healthcare Reform

"They" say that presidents as far back as Teddy Roosevelt wanted universal health care for all as a right for US citizens. During the Progressive Era, President Theodore Roosevelt (1901-1908) had the power and although he is documented as supporting health insurance for the sick because he believed that no country could be strong whose people were sick and poor, he permitted most of the initiative for reform to occur outside of government.

Who Really Is Somebody?

Emily Dickinson wrote a wonderful poem called "I'm nobody, who are you," and I must admit I love my nobodiness. This poem was a discussion point in English classes across the US in my day. Everybody had a thought on their nobodiness and their somebodiness.

I am not a Teddy Roosevelt nor am I a Teddy Kennedy. I was not a Rough Rider either but many of the rides in my life were rough. I grew up to believe that the more you have to do for yourself, the more you will be able to do for yourself and for others. The more you can do for yourself, the less likely you will have to ask your neighbor to do for you. These are the precepts that my father taught me. He was a good and fine man.

Al Jolson sang a famous song "Where Did Robinson Crusoe Go with Friday On Saturday Night." It was from 1916. Yes, music had been invented by then, actually much earlier. As you would expect, it was about Robinson Crusoe (Jolson died in 1949) and in it, the song looked at Friday, Crusoe's great pal, as a great guy. In describing Friday's greatest attributes in the song Jolson sings out, "He didn't borrow or lend."

To not borrow and to not lend was a very positive set of attributes to possess back in 1916. Isn't that interesting? The mere thought of "not working" in order to make a living was not on the table back then. Perhaps it should be taken off the table again today. Don't borrow or lend or "take" from others that which is not yours.

The worst thing that we can do for our fellow sisters and brothers is to give them all we have without them having to experience the sweat to get it. And the notion that we are all some kind of team with government as our leader makes no sense. It's un-American. We the people run this country as a group of united individuals with a common purpose—that begins with freedom from government coercion. Our common-ness may help us, but our individual purpose is a right that nobody can diminish.

We are not a pack of rats, wondering which tune the Pied Piper will play next. We are not waiting for the snake charmer du jour to charm us into taking actions that are against our individual will. I have my own will. You have your own will. It really is wonderful? Convince me if you can, but if you can't, get out of my face because I owe you nothing.

The precepts of socialism, Marxism, and communism encourage each to worship the state and to care not about individuality. I disagree intensely. I do not think it is kind to people to give them everything you have until you have nothing and they have it all. Then, in a state-run society, after giving up all of yours, your job is to ask some benefactor for kindness so that you can survive?

For some reason, government thinks of itself as the grand redistributor and this whole healthcare debacle is about redistributing your healthcare to somebody else whose care is not as good as yours. If this were a classroom, I would caution that this is not about addition or multiplication. From an individual American perspective, this is about subtraction.

Government is offering to take your healthcare insurance and give it to somebody else. If you wanted to pay for somebody else's healthcare insurance by not having your own, that is something you would be able to do without government. By the way, under the plan the government will tax you when your healthcare is gone. Who gains here other than the one who did not work for what you have?

I do not think that all or any other American or non-American has a right to my healthcare or yours or a right to anything of mine or yours. Now that we have that straight, I do think all are entitled to life, liberty and the pursuit of happiness. I wish I had thought of that. For me, all of that exists in one word -- "Freedom."

I have studied the Constitution and I know I am correct that the great founders of this country believed that government, left unchecked, would become oppressive and so, the three branches defined by the Constitution were supposed to protect us from that and more. The Founders dream has almost failed because representation has become corrupted. If things were as envisioned by the framers of the constitution, this book would not be necessary.

Like many Americans, I really do fear that the current administration is most interested in redistributing everything that you or I have to somebody who has never earned it. No, I am not for that, no matter what it is called. I see the millionaire czars, and Obama, a community organizer, also a millionaire trying to redistribute the nickels and dimes of the people. They suggest that everything you and I have should be taken from you and me and given to some poor deserving individual.

This individual will be selected by Obama and his team so that they immediately become indebted to the President and dependent on the president's good-will. That is not the country for which I signed up. Sorry Charlie! Count me out!

They will receive whether or not they have done any work to deserve anything. Neither Mr. Obama, nor his Czars, unfortunately, have bothered to include their own possessions in the giveaway. But, then again they are leaders. Yes, Virginia, we are the chopped liver.

Our dear President who cannot himself afford to have his own wealth or healthcare redistributed, has deemed that all valuables of the bourgeoisie, from healthcare to wealth should be redistributed to those in need -- the needy. Mr. Obama and his team do not always consult the Constitution as these notions are in fact quite illegal.

I am not suggesting we do not have an obligation as individuals to help our fellow man. However, I am suggesting that government has no authority to force us to be anything other than lawful citizens. Nobody, no individual, is obligated to be nice. Being a nasty S.O.B. is not against the law.

Like Jolson and Friday, another group from the fifties also delivered the meaning of this notion quite well. The Platters had it right, "To each his own." -- words and music by Jay Livingston and Ray Evans. What's yours is yours and what's mine is mine. When we go to church, I gladly give away mine and some of it may go to a particular "you" out there. That is fine because there are two in between making sure all is OK. Those two I deeply trust - My Pastor and My God. I hope that after we throw all the sleaze balls out in 2016, I may be able to trust the government again.

Even then, however, it will not be to trust them to redistribute anything of mine to anybody else. We are a country of individuals who enjoy freedom individually. We have the freedom to keep what we earn in most cases and it is no right of

government to confiscate our meager possessions so that
somebody else may enjoy them.

ER Care for All

Call me a bad guy if you want, but I don't think that illegal aliens
have any right to healthcare paid for by the good people of
America. Of course they, as well as anybody not covered, such
as visitors from other countries, should get emergency care and
any hospitalization that comes with that; however, there should
always be a bill associated with it and that bill should eventually
be paid.

I may not have friends in high places, but my friend, Captain
Mark George, at one time, a fellow faculty member at
Marywood University, and a phenomenal human being is the
head of the Aviation Program at Marywood University. He goes
pretty high!

His office was right down the hall from mine. He has a great
story about what we owe to each other. Mark would say we owe
each other life, and that means a lot to him. As a Catholic, Mark
was a bold and brazen sixteen year old and found his love life in
the process of creating a new human being. His parents helped
him know what his responsibilities were. The day I wrote this
paragraph the first time, in my office at Marywood, Mark told
me this story of his early life and then he offered me the
opportunity to interview his son, an ER surgeon in a prestigious
NY hospital. I will take him up on that one day. His love child
at 16 years old is now a trauma surgeon. Mark throws nobody
under the bus and I am proud to say I am his friend.

I have a lifetime friend, Gerry Rodski, whose baby girl at the
time was an emergency room doctor post residency in a NY
Emergency Room. She was in a different hospital than Mark's
son. From both of these professionals, working in ERs in
metropolitan cities, I know that nobody is without health care in

the US. It may not be as nice as we would like it to be for them, but they get care and then some. The idea that there is no healthcare for some is completely untrue.

The government regulations say a patient must be fed and given water if hungry and thirsty. This attracts a number of patients who otherwise would be staying outside and not eating, waiting for the next fix. From the horse's mouth, I know that batteries of tests must be performed on these poor souls if they declare that they have a real health problem, when all they really want is an extra meal or two, and an easy night's sleep.

I think we could do that with a third kind of ER, or a fourth or a fifth. Why not adjunct facilities in which a "patient" can be assured a night's rest and a few meals. We should be able to do that rather than have all the facilities of a real ER available to somebody just wanting warmth or a glass of water.

The fact is that nobody is without healthcare in America and to suggest, as I heard not too long ago that we need to spend more than a trillion dollars so that all but 25,000,000 are covered makes no sense. Even these 25,000,000 are covered in the "other" ER today or in small hospitals, in the main ER. Why should we all go broke helping people who are already being helped today? The ERs where these folks go often have two or more parallel units to give less costly care to those mandated that are really not emergencies.

Collect from the Patient

You may or may not know that the government, after mandating that the sick and the tired are cared for, tell the hospitals they have to collect from the patient. Since they can't, collect from a stone, that's the rub. Certain repeat patients know they do not have to pay so they just do not pay. Yet, the hospitals survive, because the alternative is not so attractive.

Government, unfortunately is a given. Government is almost an eternal entity that cannot die. Thus, no government employee thinks they need to work hard enough to survive, because they don't. When have you heard of a government employee being fired because they did not work hard?

I think there is no free lunch. I have said it many times in this book and every book I write. Here it is again. There is no free lunch! Somebody pays. The free lunch-crowd hopes it is not them. I like the ER system. I am amazed that the ERs can stay afloat giving care to all (in separate and unequal chambers).

That is an example of American cunning and ingenuity. Please help me understand why government running the whole show would make that better? Hospitals figured out how to survive when the government forced them to provide for all. Nobody in government, despite all who work for Uncle Sam, told them how to survive. That's the difference between the private and public sector.

Health Bills (Invoices) Should Be Accounted for Life

My perspective is that all health care bills, not otherwise covered are due -- ER and even "covered" Medicaid etc... They should be recorded permanently in an individual's record stored by a non-threatening authority (not the government). When the person is able to pay, they will know that they owe society a debt, but they will not be bugged to death.

There are millions of families in the US today harassed by call center bounty hunters trying to collect unpaid bills, often those of teenage children up to the age of 30. I would not ask that we sic such repulsive people on anybody to collect a bill, whether the person is from America, or just visiting, or even loitering. But, all ER healthcare bills are due and we, who force hospitals to be caring, need to keep track of the bills in a way that eventually, when the individual begins to prosper, they can be paid back and the money then can go to help somebody else.

Therefore, in the case of a non-citizen who is not just visiting, care providers must gain identifying information about the person as the price of health admission. It is not too much to ask for identification as all Americans must produce at care facilities. No, I am not suggesting that US Immigration and Customs Enforcement (ICE) should be called when an illegal alien comes for care.

But, I see no reason why the bill should not be kept receivable and I see no reason why the bill should ever die or be killed. Thus, we should log definitively identifying facts about everybody who gets "free ER" or any other kind of "free care," even if it is via post treatment fingerprints, so that we can post their bill to their US account.

Emergency rooms by law can deny nobody treatment, citizen or non-citizen. Yet, hospitals are not reimbursed for the cost of treatment. IMHO, that is why hospitals have had to innovate to care or go out of business. Some believe that hospitals are hurting financially because of this, and one can appreciate that without receiving due payment for services -- immediately or sometime after service, how this can be. Why anyone would deny providing ID to a hospital, is an enigma. The US Congress should get smart enough to demand it.

Hospitals do not want to eat the cost of an illegal alien or an uninsurable 26-year old who is just released from his parents insurance. They don't want to have to do three days a week tests on the same person under different non-IDs when that person is really looking for a soup kitchen and a night shelter. Hospitals should not have to eat the cost for anybody getting service and not paying.

Yet they do and they make do, but barely, and that is why this type of service is not bankrupting America. There is no room for fat. I propose that we capture the patient billing data in a huge database and keep the bill due forever until the patient dies. Then, we should be able to get as much as possible from the estate. No, ICE should not be able to see the records, but a second or third trip to the ER over the years by a non-citizen should have consequences.

Who Pays?

American citizens do not want to have to pay for other citizens to get healthcare or they would be hanging out at Emergency rooms with their wallets opened, giving away cash. When have you done that?

You do not want to pay for the guy down the street and the guy down the street does not want to pay for you. Healthcare is no different from anything else. You want ice cream, you pay for it. The guy down the street does not buy yours and you do not buy the ice cream for the guy down the street.

Once anybody, legal or illegal, gets healthcare under any means from the US government or from a provider under government mandate, that bill should become due and should stay due even if the government or some other entity pays for it, initially to make the provider whole.

Check the Bible and check the Constitution. Receiving stolen property doesn't cut it in either book.

This chapter is about the second big healthcare debate of my lifetime. I have already given you an awful lot of facts, as I have studied this for a long time. But there are a lot more facts and perspectives to be shared.

Nobody has a right to the property of anybody else. It really does not matter if a third party like government is used to confiscate and deliver the property or the ultimate receiver of the property steals it themselves. Both are sins of theft in my opinion and neither leads to a productive mentality in a nation's people/ workforce.

It is not good for the "giver" and it is not good for the getter. The reason for the quotes around the word giver is that it is really not given, it is taken. I most certainly believe in charity. I believe in giving charity and I believe in taking charity when it is needed. I do not believe, however, in governments' role as an honest broker middleman.

Politicians have ulterior motives like buying votes and I think that if politicians want to buy votes, they should do so with their own money. I do not believe that you should decide my fair charitable share, nor I yours.

Chapter 11   Year Six of the Affordable Care Act

Obamacare's Mounting Problems

Selections in this chapter have been taken from the Heritage Foundation's Groundbreaking work. I strongly recommend your joining the Heritage Foundation for the good of America.

Founded in 1973, The Heritage Foundation is a research and educational institution—a think tank—whose mission is to formulate and promote conservative public policies based on the principles of free enterprise, limited government, individual freedom, traditional American values, and a strong national defense.

Dr. Robert Moffit of The Heritage Foundation shows the six-year history of Obamacare in a fashion that is both comprehensive and comprehensible. Rather than attempt to rewrite this history in my own pen, I have used his thorough analysis to present the facts and make the argument that Obamacare is a law ready made for repeal.

Brian W. Kelly

Year Six of the Affordable Care Act(2016): Obamacare's Mounting Problems

By Robert E. Moffit, Ph.D.
A Senior Fellow Center for Health Policy Studies

The Affordable Care Act (ACA, popularly known as Obamacare) is ripe for repeal. For the American public, there are ample reasons for dissatisfaction: higher costs; arbitrary and sometimes absurd rulemaking; bureaucratization of an already overly bureaucratized sector of the economy; incompatibility with personal freedom and religious liberty; enormous spending and heavy taxation; and widely acknowledged design flaws, evident in the ACA's hopelessly complex and unworkable subsidy schemes, boondoggle bailouts, and collapsing co-ops.

For many Americans, opposition to the ACA is rightly rooted in their rejection of the tacit assumption underlying its centralized architecture: that the political class possesses the wit and wisdom to restrain, guide, and direct this enormously complex and dynamic sector of the American economy and, in pursuit of that project, must exert greater control over their personal lives. Americans know that their elected representatives can craft a much better alternative than periodically patching the flawed Affordable Care Act.

Key Points

- ✓ Despite the President's repeated promises, rising insurance costs under the Affordable Care Act continue to burden businesses and families.

- ✓ The ACA has reduced insurance competition and has a negative impact on job growth.

- ✓ The overall health care cost curve is "bending" upward, not downward as advocates promised.

✓ The ACA is imposing major tax increases on America's middle class.

✓ Medicare payment cuts threaten seniors' future access to care.

✓ The ACA forces Americans, in direct violation of their rights of conscience, to fund abortion through their tax dollars.

✓ Beyond the ACA, federal health policies governing the pre-Obamacare health care arrangements, particularly the insurance markets, were profoundly flawed.

✓ The task for Congress is now to present and promote a new vision and craft the legislative details necessary to fulfill it.

Americans are engaged in an intense national debate over the Patient Protection and Affordable Care Act of 2010 (ACA, popularly known as "Obamacare"). Despite President Barack Obama's glowing account of his "signature" accomplishment, the ACA's six-year record demonstrates that the legislative product he signed into law is deeply—and in many respects irreparably—flawed. Obamacare is bedeviled by poor performance in a number of vital areas:

1. Increased costs for individuals, families, and businesses;
2. Resumption of excessive health care spending and middle-class taxation; and
3. A seemingly endless series of managerial failures or unanticipated consequences.

The ACA is a formidable engine of concentrated bureaucratic power and control, yet its future is clouded by persistent unpopularity.

My sincere thank you from all of us to Robert E. Moffit, PhD, a Senior Fellow in the Center for Health Policy Studies, of the Institute for Family, Community, and Opportunity, at The Heritage Foundation.

Appendix A

From the Internet -- Letter to Glen Beck

This letter is the greatest summary I can give about how America feels about Obama's Seven Deadly Sins

From: Loyal American
Date: Wed, 4 Nov 2009 20:46:03 -0500
Subject: BRAVO x 1,000,000,000!!!!!!!!!!!

The following letter read on Glenn Beck's show, is rapidly circulating around the country. Americans everywhere identify with this 53-year-old woman. She has given us a voice. Once you read this, you will want to forward it to all of your friends...

GLENN BECK: I got a letter from a woman in Arizona. She writes an open letter to our nation's leadership:

"I am a home grown American citizen, 53, registered Democrat all my life. Before the last presidential election I registered as a Republican because I no longer felt the Democratic Party represents my views or works to pursue issues important to me. Now I no longer feel the Republican Party represents my views or works to pursue issues important to me. The fact is I no longer feel any political party or representative in Washington represents my views or works to pursue the issues important to me. Instead, we are burdened with Congressional Dukes and Duchesses who think they know better than the citizens they are supposed to represent.

There must be someone. Please tell me who you are. Please stand up and tell me that you are there and that you're willing to fight for our Constitution as it was written. Please stand up now.

You might ask yourself what my views and issues are that I would feel so horribly disenfranchised by both major political parties. What kind of nut-job am I? Well, these briefly are the views and issues for which I seek representation:

One, illegal immigration. I want you to stop coddling illegal immigrants and secure our borders. Close the underground tunnels. Stop the violence and the trafficking in drugs and people. No amnesty, not again. Been there, done that, no resolution. P.S., I'm not a racist. This is not to be confused with legal immigration.

Two, the STIMULUS bill. I want it repealed and I want no further funding supplied to it. We told you No, but you did it anyway. I want the remaining unfunded 95% repealed. Freeze, repeal.

Three: Czars. I want the circumvention of our constitutional checks and balances stopped immediately. Fire the czars. No more czars. Government officials answer to the process, not to the president. Stop trampling on our Constitution, and honor it.

Four, cap and trade. The debate on global warming is not over. There are many conflicting opinions and it is too soon for this radical legislation. Quit throwing our nation into politically-correct quicksand.

Five, universal healthcare. I will not be rushed into another expensive decision that will burden me, my children, and grandchildren. Don't you dare try to pass this in the middle of the night without even reading it. Slow down! Fix only what is broken -- we have the best health care system in the world -- and test any new program in one or two states first.

Six, growing government control. I want states' rights and sovereignty fully restored. I want less government in my life, not more. More is not better! Shrink it down. Mind your own business. You have enough to take care of with your real [Constitutional] obligations. Why don't you start there?

Seven, ACORN. I do not want ACORN and its affiliates in charge of our 2010 census. I want them investigated. I also do not want mandatory escrow fees contributed to them every time on every real estate deal that closes -- how did they pull that one off? Stop the funding to ACORN and its affiliates pending impartial audits and investigations. I do not trust them with taking the census with our taxpayer money. I don't trust them with any of our taxpayer money. Face up to the allegations against them and get it resolved before taxpayers get any more involved with them. If it walks like a duck and talks like a duck, hello. Stop protecting your political buddies. You work for us, the people. Investigate.

Eight, redistribution of wealth. No, no, no. I work for my money. It is mine. I have always worked for people with more money than I have because they gave me jobs -- and that is the only redistribution of wealth that I will support. I never got a job from a poor person! Why do you want me to hate my employers? And what do you have against shareholders making a profit?

Nine, charitable contributions. Although I never got a job from a poor person, I have helped many in need. Charity belongs in our local communities, where we know our needs best and can use our local talent and our local resources. Butt out, please. We want to do it ourselves.

Ten, corporate bailouts. Knock it off. Every company must sink or swim like the rest of us. If there are hard times ahead, we'll be better off just getting into it and letting the strong survive. Quick and painful. (Have you ever ripped off a Band-Aid?) We will pull together. Great things happen in America under great hardship. Give us the chance to innovate. We cannot disappoint you more than you have disappointed us.

Eleven, transparency and accountability. How about it? No, really, how about it? Let's have it. Let's say we give the buzzwords a rest and have some straight honest talk. Please stop trying to manipulate and appease me with clever wording. I am not the idiot you obviously take me for. Stop sneaking around and meeting in back rooms making deals with your friends. It will only be a prelude to your criminal investigation. Stop hiding things from me.

Twelve, unprecedented quick spending. Stop it now.
Take a breath. Listen to the people. Slow down and get some input from nonpoliticians and experts on the subject. Stop making everything an emergency. Stop speed-reading our bills into law. I am not an activist. I am not a community organizer. Nor am I a terrorist, a militant or a violent person. I am a parent and a grandparent. I work. I'm busy. I am busy, and I am tired. I thought we elected competent people to take care of the business of government so that we could work, raise our families, pay our bills, have a little recreation, complain about taxes, endure our hardships, pursue our personal goals, cut our lawn, wash our cars on the weekends and be responsible contributing members of society and teach our children to be the same all while living in the home of the free and land of the brave.

I entrusted you with upholding the Constitution. I believed in the checks and balances to keep from getting far off course. What happened? You are very far off course. Do you really think I find humor in the hiring of a speed reader to unintelligently ramble all through a bill that you signed into law without knowing what it contained? I do not.

It is a mockery of the responsibility I have entrusted to you. It is a slap in the face. I am not laughing at your arrogance. Why is it that I feel as if you would not trust me to make a single decision about my own life and how I would live it but you should expect that I should trust you with the debt that you have laid on all of us and our children? We did not want the TARP bill. We said no. We would repeal it if we could. I am sure that we still cannot. There is needless urgency and recklessness in all of your recent spending of our tax dollars.

From my perspective, it seems that all of you have gone insane. I also know that I am far from alone in these feelings. Do you honestly feel that your current pursuits have merit to patriotic Americans? We want it to stop. We want to put the brakes on everything that is being rushed by us and forced upon us. We want our voice back. You have forced us to put our lives on hold to straighten out the mess that you are making. We will have to give up our vacations, our time spent with our children, any relaxation time we may have had and money we cannot afford to spend on bringing our concerns to Washington. Our president often knows all the right buzzwords like unsustainable. Well, no kidding. How many tens of thousands of dollars did the focus group cost to come up with that word? We don't want your overpriced words. Stop treating us like we're morons.

We want all of you to stop focusing on your reelection and do the job we want done, not the job you want done or the job your party wants done. You work for us and at this rate I guarantee you not for long because we are coming. We will be heard and we will be represented.. You think we're so busy with our lives that we will never come for you? We are the formerly silent majority, all of us who quietly work, pay taxes, obey the law, vote, save money, keep our noses to the grindstone... and we are now looking at you.

You have awakened us, the patriotic freedom spirit so strong and so powerful that it had been sleeping too long. You have pushed us too far. Our numbers are great. They may surprise you. For every one of us who will be there, there will be hundreds more that could not come. Unlike you, we have their trust. We will represent them honestly, rest assured. They will be at the polls on voting day to usher you out of office.

We have cancelled vacations. We will use our last few dollars saved. We will find the representation among us and a grassroots campaign will flourish. We didn't ask for this fight. But the gloves are coming off. We do not come in violence, but we are angry. You will represent us or you will be replaced with someone who will. There are candidates among us who will rise like a Phoenix from the ashes that you have made of our constitution.

Democrat, Republican, independent, libertarian. Understand this. We don't care. Political parties are meaningless to us Patriotic Americans are willing to do right by us and our Constitution, and that is all that matters to us now. We are going to fire all of you who abuse power and seek more. It is not your power. It is ours and we want it back. We entrusted you with it and you abused it. You are dishonorable. You are dishonest. As Americans we are ashamed of you. You have brought shame to us. If you are not representing the wants and needs of your constituency loudly and consistently, in spite of the objections of your party, you will be fired. Did you hear? We no longer care about your political parties. You need to be loyal to us, not to them... Because we will get you fired and they will not save you.

If you do or can represent me, my issues, my views, please stand up. Make your identity known. You need to make some noise about it. Speak up. I need to know who you are. If you do not speak up, you will be herded out with the rest of the sheep and we will replace the whole damn congress if need be one by one. We are coming. Are we coming for you?

Who do you represent? What do you represent? Listen. Because we are coming. We the people are coming.

Appendix B

From the Internet -- List of Obama Failures- Updated and Getting Worse By the Day!

http://www.martinoauthor.com/list-obama-failures/

"The Obama administration has been marred by debt, scandals, foreign policy failures, and an overall fragmentation of this country. He has plunged the United States into an abyss of economic debt that will create generations of American servitude paying off his wayward spending endeavors. The Red, White and Blue's epitaph will read like a litany of failures perpetrated on both the American people and the world by this president:

Photo supplied by Stephen Martino www.martinoauthor.com

Scandals:

- ✓ IRS targets Obama's enemies
- ✓ Benghazi
- ✓ Spying on the AP
- ✓ The ATF "Fast and Furious" scheme
- ✓ Sebelius demands payment
- ✓ The Pigford Agriculture Department Scandal
- ✓ The General Services Administration Las Vegas Spending Spree.
- ✓ Veterans Affairs in Disney World and neglecting vets
- ✓ Solyndra
- ✓ New Black Panthers Voter Intimidation
- ✓ The hacking of Sharyl Attkisson's computer
- ✓ Obama's LIES about the Affordable Care Act
- ✓ "I'll Pass My Own Laws"
- ✓ NSA Spying on American People

Foreign Policy

- ✓ Lack of solidarity with Israel
- ✓ Disaster with the Arab Spring
- ✓ Crimea
- ✓ Leaving Iraq too soon and letting ISIS take over
- ✓ Handling of Syrian Red Line
- ✓ Calling ISIS "JV"
- ✓ Failing to Recognize ISIS as a Radical (or Devout) Muslim Movement
- ✓ Returning the bust of Churchill to the Brits
- ✓ Lack of Confidence by NATO nations
- ✓ Signing a Disastrous Nuclear Deal with the Mullahs of Iran
- ✓ Paid $5 Billion & Released 5 Taliban Prisoners for Deserter Bergdahl

- ✓ Waging war -- attacking Libya w/o Congressional approval
- ✓ Allowed new Chinese bases in the South China Sea and off the coast of Somalia at the entrance to the gulf of Aden
- ✓ Paying ransom to Iranian for hostages- and using foreign currency in unmarked plane

Domestic Policy

- ✓ Failure to secure the Border
- ✓ Illegals bringing guns, drug and diseases through the southern border
- ✓ Passing on the keystone pipeline
- ✓ 9 Trillion dollars more in debt
- ✓ Vast expansion of government
- ✓ Racial Division at all-time high
- ✓ Inviting Bomb Boy Ahmed to White House
- ✓ Disrespect for Cops
- ✓ Failed economic stimulus plan
- ✓ Constant disregard for the Constitution and tyrannical rule
- ✓ China overtook America as world's largest economy

Double Downgrade

- ✓ Housing policies failed to stop foreclosures
- ✓ Price of healthcare has drastically risen for those purchasing it
- ✓ Education policies failed to curb college costs
- ✓ Highest percentage of Americans on Food Stamps and Medicaid
- ✓ Record 92,898,000 Americans over 16 years not working
- ✓ Lowest Labor Force participation rate of 62.7%
- ✓ Denying the notion of American Exceptionalism
- ✓ Not Securing the Olympics for Chicago in 2016
- ✓ Naming numerous Communists/Socialists/Progressives to Czar Positions

- ✓ Mismanagement and cover up of Terrorist shootings in San Bernardino, California
- ✓ Mismanagement of Gulf Oil Spill
- ✓ Disastrous Vetting Process of "Immigrants" from Muslim Nations

The above list provided by author Stephen Martino from his web site. Help him out by buying his new Conservative, Political/Sci-Fi Thriller titled: THE HIDDEN REALITY

Note from Stephen Martino:

I stand by the list I've created. Obama has decimated the Constitution, made us a country of dependents, weakened the economy, further created a foreign affairs nightmare, made our country unsafe, turned on the police, spied on Americans, and golfed his way through the past 7 years.

Newt Gingrich Weighs In!

Former Speaker of the House Newt Gingrich has taken on President Obama in all of his eight years and finds the President having committed far more than seven deadly sins.

In early August 2016 on Hannity, for example, the Speaker went off on President Obama for urging Republican leaders to withdraw support for Donald Trump and calling the GOP nominee "unfit to serve."

Gingrich said that it was "pretty despicable for a President of the United States to be that harsh about his potential successor." "I mean, talk about undermining the United States of America, President Obama potentially did that today."

Gingrich also went off on Obama for criticizing Trump for not knowing things when the president was wrong on a host of damaging issues such as keeping your doctor under Obamacare, red lines in Syria, Russia taking Crimea, Iraq collapsing and Chicago murders.

"You go down the list of things Barack Obama doesn't know and it is astonishing the arrogance and the demagoguery of this man in just sweeping away others. I think that the Obama presidency will be looked back upon as one of the great failures in American history."

Add all that to the seven deadly sins and many more; and we the people have simply had a miserable eight years with a President that we have become convinced does not even like America.

LETS GO PUBLISH! Books by Brian Kelly:

(sold at www.bookhawkers.com Amazon.com, and Kindle.).

LETS GO PUBLISH! is proud to announce that more AS/400 and Power i books are becoming available to help you inexpensively address your AS/400 and Power i education and training needs: Our general titles precede specific AS/400 and other technology books. Check out these great patriotic books which precede the tech books in the list.

101 Secrets How to be a High Information Voter
You do not have to be a low-information voter.

Why Trump?
You Already Know... But, this book will tell you anyway

Saving America The Trump Way!
A book that tells you how President Donald Trump will help Merica dn Americans wind up on top

The US Immigration Fix
It's all in here. You won't want to put it down

I had a Dream IBM Could be #1 Again
The title is self-explanatory

Whatever Happened to the IBM AS/400?
The question is answered in this nee book.

Great Moments in Penn State Football Check out the particulars of this great
book at bookhawkers.com.

Great Moments in Notre Dame Football Check out the particulars of this great
book at bookhawkers.com or www.notredamebooks.com

WineDiets.Com Presents The Wine Diet Learn how to lose weight while having
fun. Four specific diets and some great anecdotes fill this book with fun and the opportunity to lose weight in the process.

Wilkes-Barre, PA; Return to Glory Wilkes-Barre City's return to glory begins with
dreams and ideas. Along with plans and actions, this equals leadership.

The Lifetime Guest Plan. This is a plan which if deployed today would
immediately solve the problem of 60 million illegal aliens in the United States.

Geoffrey Parsons' Epoch... The Land of Fair Play Better than the original. The
greatest re-mastering of the greatest book ever written on American Civics. It was built for all Americans as the best govt. design in the history of the world.

The Bill of Rights 4 Dummmies! This is the best book to learn about your rights.
Be the first, to have a "Rights Fest" on your block. You will win for sure!

Sol Bloom's Epoch ...Story of the Constitution This work by Sol Bloom was
written to commemorate the Sesquicentennial celebration of the Constitution. It has been remastered by Lets Go Publish! – An excellent read!

The Constitution 4 Dummmies! This is the best book to learn about the
Constitution. Learn all about the fundamental laws of America.

America for Dummmies!
All Americans should read to learn about this great country.

Just Say No to Chris Christie for President two editions – I & II
Discusses the reasons why Chris Christie is a poor choice for US President

The Federalist Papers by Hamilton, Jay, Madison w/ intro by Brian Kelly
Complete unabridged, easier to read version of the original Federalist Papers

Companion to Federalist Papers by Hamilton, Jay, Madison w/ intro by Brian Kelly
This small, inexpensive book will help you navigate the Federalist Papers

Kill the Republican Party! (2013 edition and edition #2)
Demonstrates why the Republican Party must be abandoned by conservatives

Bring On the American Party!
Demonstrates how conservatives can be free from the party of wimps by starting its own national party called the American Party.

No Amnesty! No Way!
In addition to describing the issue in detail, this book also offers a real solution.

Saving America
This how-to book is about saving our country using strong mercantilist principles. These same principles that helped the country from its founding.

RRR:
A unique plan for economic recovery and job creation

Kill the EPA
The EPA seems to hate mankind and love nature. They are also making it tough for asthmatics to breathe and for those with malaria to live. It's time they go.

Obama's Seven Deadly Sins.
In the Obama Presidency, there are many concerns about the long-term prospects and sustainability of the country. We examine each of the President's seven deadliest sins in detail, offering warnings and a number of solutions. Be careful. Book may nudge you to move to Canada or Europe.

Taxation Without Representation Second Edition
At the time of the Boston Tea Party, there was no representation. Now, there is no representation again but there are "representatives."

Healthcare Accountability
Who should pay for your healthcare? Whose healthcare should you pay for? Is it a lifetime free ride on others or should those once in need of help have to pay it back when their lives improve?

Jobs! Jobs! Jobs!
Where have all the American Jobs gone and how can we get them back?

Other IBM I Technical Books

The All Everything Operating System:
Story about IBM's finest operating system; its facilities; how it came to be.

The All-Everything Machine
Story about IBM's finest computer server.

Chip Wars
The story of ongoing wars between Intel and AMD and upcoming wars between Intel and IBM. Book may cause you to buy / sell somebody's stock.

Can the AS/400 Survive IBM?
Exciting book about the AS/400 in a System i5 World.

The IBM i Pocket SQL Guide.
Complete Pocket Guide to SQL as implemented on System i5. A must have for SQL developers new to System i5. It is very compact yet very comprehensive and it is example driven. Written in a part tutorial and part reference style, Tons of SQL coding samples, from the simple to the sublime.

The IBM i Pocket Query Guide.
If you have been spending money for years educating your Query users, and you find you are still spending, or you've given up, this book is right for you. This one QuikCourse covers all Query options.

The IBM I Pocket RPG & RPG IV Guide.
Comprehensive RPG & RPGIV Textbook -- Over 900 pages. This is the one RPG book to have if you are not having more than one. All areas of the language covered smartly in a convenient sized book Annotated PowerPoint's available for self-study (extra fee for self-study package)

The IBM I RPG Tutorial and Lab Guide – Recently Revised.
Your guide to a hands-on Lab experience. Contains CD with Lab exercises and PowerPoint's. Great companion to the above textbook or can be used as a standalone for student Labs or tutorial purposes

The IBM i Pocket Developers' Guide.
Comprehensive Pocket Guide to all of the AS/400 and System i5 development tools - DFU, SDA, etc. You'll also get a big bonus with chapters on Architecture, Work Management, and Subfile Coding.

The IBM i Pocket Database Guide.
Complete Pocket Guide to System i5 integrated relational database (DB2/400) – physical and logical files and DB operations - Union, Projection, Join, etc. Written in a part tutorial and part reference style. Tons of DDS coding samples.

Getting Started with The WebSphere Development Studio Client for System i5 (WDSc).
Focus is on client server and the Web. Includes CODE/400, VisualAge RPG, CGI, WebFacing, and WebSphere Studio. Case study continues from the Interactive Book.

The System i5 Pocket WebFacing Primer.
This book gets you started immediately with WebFacing. A sample case study is used as the basis for a conversion to WebFacing. Interactive 5250 application is WebFaced in a case study form before your eyes.

Getting Started with WebSphere Express Server for IBM i Step-by-Step Guide for Setting up Express Servers
A comprehensive guide to setting up and using WebSphere Express. It is filled with examples, and structured in a tutorial fashion for easy learning.

The WebFacing Application Design & Development Guide:
Step by Step Guide to designing green screen IBM i apps for the Web. Both a systems design guide and a developers guide. Book helps you understand how to design and develop Web applications using regular RPG or COBOL programs.

The System i5 Express Web Implementer's Guide.
Your one stop guide to ordering, installing, fixing, configuring, and using WebSphere Express, Apache, WebFacing, System i5 Access for Web, and HATS/LE.

Joomla! Technical Books
Best Damn Joomla Tutorial Ever
Learn Joomla! By example.

Best Damn Joomla Intranet Tutorial Ever
This book is the only book that shows you how to use Joomla on a corporate intranet.

Best Damn Joomla Template Tutorial Ever
This book teaches you step-by step how to work with templates in Joomla!

Best Damn Joomla Installation Guide Ever
Teaches you how to install Joomla! On all major platforms besides IBM i.

Best Damn Blueprint for Building Your Own Corporate Intranet.
This excellent timeless book helps you design a corporate intranet for any platform while using Joomla as its basis.
4
IBM i PHP & MySQL Installation & Operations Guide
How to install and operate Joomla! on the IBM i Platform

IBM i PHP & MySQL Programmers Guide
programs for IBM i

* 9 7 8 0 9 9 7 7 6 6 7 8 3 *